Feeding Your
Anorexic Adolescent

Claire P. Norton, M.S., R.D.

Copyright 2009

Claire P. Norton M.S.,R.D.

Nutritpress

USA

Nutripress@nutripressusa.com

Library of Congress

Cataloging-in Publication Data

ISBN 978-1-60743-791-8

Acknowlegements

I would like to thank the many colleagues and friends who have made this book a reality. Deb Napier and Julie Marcus who showed me what my book would look like when it was still a dream. Laura Koenigs, Nancy Miller, Beth Russell-Smith, Janice Jones and Pat Donovan for reading and editing the early manuscripts. Laura Collins and Dr. James Lock for taking the time to read my book and make valuable comments. Eddie Goldberg for his careful editing. Joshua Goldstein for his patient and unfailing belief that this book should be published. Thanks to you and to the many families I have had the pleasure of working with – all of you are here in this book. Lastly, a big thanks to my wonderful children, Paul, Kevin and Caroline who tested my recipes.

Preface – Note to Readers

This book is not meant to take the place of medical advice. Rather it is meant as a resource for adolescents using family based therapy for treatment of their adolescent's eating disorder. Eating disorders are serious illnesses and should be treated as soon as possible for the best outcomes.

Table of Contents

Recipes

Resources for Parents

Introduction

I first met Nick when he was 13 years old. A straight "A" student, somewhat shy, he was immediately likeable. A swimmer, very tall for his age, he was handsome and very thin. Nick was suffering from anorexia nervosa. At 5'9" he weighed 113 pounds, He should have weighed 127 pounds and was 125 pounds before the onset of his illness. His heart rate on his first visit to the clinic was very low.

Nick's history is somewhat typical of the stories we hear in our clinic. He started to watch his diet after a discussion of "bad" fats during health class. This "healthy eating" phase quickly became an obsession and Nick started to lose weight. Along with weight loss came a dramatic change in behavior. Nick started checking all nutrition labels, he avoided all fats and sweet foods including ice cream. It became obvious to his parents that Nick was in trouble and that this diet had gone terribly wrong.

Worried and refusing to send their son to a residential treatment center, they found our clinic, where he could receive treatment while living at home. They didn't want to send him away to a residential treatment program given that he was only

13. This had been the recommendation before they found our clinic and the Maudsley approach.

When I met his parents in our clinic, they were very anxious and unsure of how to proceed. With support and guidance they successfully guided their son toward recovery, and five months after they started treatment Nick was at a normal weight. His treatment continued until he was eating all the foods he had eaten before the eating disorder. Therapy continued to make sure he was walking the path from adolescence to adulthood with the very best of communication skills and emotional resilience. When I saw Nick six months later, his weight was in a perfect range and he was growing and developing normally. He is still tall and is now even more handsome!

Here are are some of the comments his mother made about their experience using the Maudsley method:

> "One of the greatest benefits of the Maudsley method, which we found with every professional we encountered during treatment, was the fact that no one tried to waste time figuring out how or why my son developed an eating disorder or whose "fault" it was. I could have come up with a list of at least 20 possible contributing factors as to why this happened—from genes, the proper alignment of the sun, moon, and stars, to my son's internally driven personality or the inevitable stress of his older twin brothers' college searches that year—but I knew agonizing over how much or if each factor contributed was pointless. The prevailing attitude from the first treatment visit to the last was, 'Regardless of how we got here, let's move forward and see what we can do about fixing it.' Maudsley was a positive,

encouraging experience and allowed for occasional ups and downs in progress."

"The 'eating disorder' was viewed as a separate entity from my son, and he was taught to eventually realize that. It was the 'eating disorder' that made him think a certain way or uncharacteristically lie about how much exercise he had done. Initially, the 'eating disorder' overpowered him, and that's why he was not allowed to make food decisions. By the time he began over-powering the 'eating disorder,' we all actually felt a little like we had won a victory or conquered an enemy."

My part in Nick's recovery was, in the scheme of things, small. I am a nutritionist who is dedicated to helping teenagers with eating disorders. I do this by helping their parents figure out how to achieve their goal of restoring weight onto their previously robust but now physically fragile children. I have the good luck to work alongside therapists trained in the Maudsley method, which has been proven to be more effective, faster, and have longer lasting results than individual therapy in which the adolescent is brought to talk to a therapist about their eating disorder while the worried parents sit in the waiting room.

I coach parents as they implement the Maudsley method of treatment which requires that they start feeding their children to restore them to good health. I give practical suggestions about how this can be done. More from Nick's mother:

"Just some of the benefits we received from the dietician (Most of those relating to food were with everyday items around the house. Thank goodness none required exceptional cooking ability.):

o   Lists of plenty of snack choices

o   Recipes that were high calorie and high protein
o   Simple ideas like adding certain sauces or knowing which foods were particularly beneficial
o   Several articles and web sites about normal eating, eating disorders, and the Maudsley method
o   Advice on the nutritional needs of a growing, athletic adolescent boy (a 6-foot middle schooler), both while recovering from an eating disorder and after recovery
o   Specific suggestions that he could tell himself when he worried about his eating in comparison to his peers
o   Simple 'scientific' or 'biological' explanations to questions or concerns when warranted, which were helpful in motivating my academic son to improve his health
o   Once he was doing better, a useful hunger scale with info on where he should be before and after eating, and how he might physically feel at each place on the scale. Even now, it is still useful to think about occasionally."

The Maudsley approach is new, and it is different from what has gone on in the past. Historically, in the U.S., adolescents with eating disorders have been treated apart from their families, either in individual therapy or through hospitalization. The belief that the family was a part of the pathology of the eating disorder meant that parents were advised to relinquish control of feeding their children to professionals experienced in the field of eating disorders.

Our clinic is one of a growing number of centers in the

United States that is using Maudsley therapy to treat eating disorders. This therapy depends on the parent-child relationship to treat these adolescents and children. Children are treated while they live at home, and the family unites with the child to fight the eating disorder.

Research results are very favorable and show that involved parents who use such a family-based approach are more successful in achieving permanent recovery for their children. This recovery takes place at home with the parents in charge. The name "Maudsley" comes from the hospital in England where the therapy was first used. The process is described for parents in the book "Help Your Teenager Beat an Eating Disorder" by Lock and le Grange. (See Books, page 187, for more books that describe Maudsley therapy.)

In Maudsley therapy the family is seen as a resource, and its strength is used to fight the eating disorder. The parents are told that treating the eating disorder has to be a high priority in the family. In our clinic we compare it to a diagnosis of cancer: potentially fatal if not treated. In the Maudsley approach no one is to blame for the eating disorder, neither the parents nor the child. The family is encouraged to feel strong in the face of the eating disorder. Food is seen as medicine and is as important as any other medicine when trying to cure a disease.

Many parents have heard that eating disorders are caused by their teenager "needing more control," and they are afraid that by confronting their child's diminishing intake they will make it worse. They blame themselves and feel that somehow they have caused it by insisting on healthy eating or wanting a child to exercise and be fit. Maudsley therapy shows them this is not the case. Guilt is disabling, so when you fully believe that you did not cause the disorder then you will be stronger to fight it. Fighting will require strength, resolve, and determination because eating disorders do not skulk away; they leave kicking and screaming.

Maudsley therapy shows that it is within the family, with the support and guidance of a therapist or team, that your child will recover. The approach is very specific about how this should happen and the therapy is divided into three stages. The first stage is the weight restoration phase, in which all energy goes into interrupting the eating disorder behaviors. The second stage involves renegotiating the control of food and slowly handing this back to the now normal-weight child. The last stage involves therapy around normal adolescent development and maximizing communication patterns within the family.

With Maudsley therapy your knowledge of your child is used to help in recovery. We know that you know your child best. The therapy uses the trust between parents and children, built up over years of parenting, to fight the disorder that can so brutally disrupt the parent-child relationship. Your opinion will be needed and valued. In previous therapies for adolescent eating disorders, parents were asked to step aside and let the "experts" take care of their children. With Maudsley therapy you are in charge, with the help of people who understand eating disorders and who have helped other families recover. Again, I would refer you to the excellent book by Lock and le Grange, "Help Your Teenager Beat an Eating Disorder."

Having worked with many parents during this process, I feel that they need as much support as possible as they encourage their child to eat and gain weight. I have written this book in an attempt to relieve some of the stress experienced during the initial stages of recovery. This book provides parents with practical ideas for implementing the family-based therapy plan. It gives logistical support and high-calorie recipes as well as background information about the physiology of under-nutrition and weight restoration. Recovery happens one spoonful at a time with supportive parents acting as coach, cheerleader, therapist, high-calorie cook, and shoulder to cry on.

I have found that children with eating disorders can obsess about food and food choices. It is a good idea to lessen their involvement in family cooking as much as possible. This will involve keeping them out of the kitchen during food preparation if that is what it takes. I would not discuss the contents of this book or the recipes with your child. This will over-involve them in food choices and recipe ideas that may be scary for them. Save your energy for the task of actual weight restoration, and not the discussion of the nutritional value of a food or recipes. Some parents have found that giving a child a choice can be helpful. For example, "Do you want a chicken pot pie or mushroom chicken one night this week?"

One of my patient's parents, on a follow-up visit, asked me if I had a good, on-line calorie counting resource. I asked her why on earth she needed that. She replied that she had been spending a lot of time working out the calories for each meal. I did not give her a good on-line resource. I told her to stop counting calories. I actually know the calorie content of the recipes in this book, but they are not included for a reason. You do not need to count calories. Just use your parental judgment. The weight gain (or lack of weight gain) will tell you if you are on the right track. Your time is better spent persuading your child to eat, or if you get a chance, relaxing!

Knowledge is power. It is my hope that this book will empower you as you help your child restore their weight. I believe that parents are the experts on choosing which strategy will best suit their child, and which foods will be the easiest and hardest to persuade their children to eat. I also believe that a lot of stress can be avoided by using the experience of others in the same situation as you now find yourself. My book is an attempt to put ideas that other parents have found useful at your fingertips.

Parents need to be united in working against the eating disorder. This will strengthen the force working against it. Both parents need to be involved and present a consistent message. I have noticed in my work with families that many times it is the mother that bears a lot of the work of weight restoration. Over the long term it is very hard for one person to battle their adolescent's eating disorder on their own. Make sure that both of you (the parents) feel committed and strong in battling the eating disorder together.

My book has many practical meal ideas, as well as recipes. Some are my own and some are gleaned from friends and family. High in calories and protein, they are examples of good recipes for weight restoration. However, they are only examples. There are thousands of recipes that could be used. You have, I am sure, many family recipes that would also meet the needs of your child. You can use the recipes in this book to cook by, or simply use them as a guide in choosing which of your own recipes to use. Either way, I hope they are useful.

It is my sincere wish that this book takes away even a small piece of your stress and helps you get through this difficult and crucial time in your child's life.

For simplicity I have used "she" and "her" instead of "she/he," "him/her," or "them/their." I have worked with both boys and girls who have eating disorders and the ideas in this book are not gender-specific.

In summary

A new treatment called Maudsley or family-based therapy, which uses the family to treat a child or adolescent with anorexia is now being used in many treatment centers across the U.S. This is a complete turnaround from the older recommendation of sending even young adolescents and children away to treatment centers. In this approach families are not blamed for the illness but rather are seen as a resource on the road to recovery. This book gives parents recipes and practical ideas to help implement the treatment plan outlined by Maudsley therapy.

You may encounter many defeats

but you must not be defeated.

In fact, it may be necessary to encounter the defeats,

so you can know who you are,

what you can rise from,

how you can still come out of it.

Maya Angelou

Getting Started

This book assumes that you have chosen a family-therapy approach to treating your child's eating disorder. I will spend a little time explaining the roles of the people who will participate in your child's recovery. The most important player is, of course, the family. Each family member will have a role in your child's recovery. You, as parents, will need to assume control over your child's eating. Your other children will be helpful too, as they have seen the impact of the disorder on their sibling and on the family as a whole. They will be expected to contribute, not as parents assuming control over their sibling's food intake, but as someone to hang out and relax with. The other people who help in the recovery are a physician and a therapist. Some families also have the benefit of a nutritionist as a type of coach in this process.

Each of the care team members has a specific role in the treatment plan, and all work together to help in the recovery process. The role of the team is to guide the progress of the patient. It is important for parents to know that an eating disorder clinic is a safe place for them and their children. Professionals working independently also can cooperate closely to provide the support needed. Be sure that the professionals you have chosen have experience with eating disorders and can provide the kind of support you will need using a Maudsley based family-therapy approach.

Role of the Physician

The physician is usually the first team member to see a child with an eating disorder. The physician will conduct a complete physical examination of your child to rule out any medical cause for the weight loss. When a diagnosis of an eating disorder is made, the physician will look for any signs of physical distress caused by the eating disorder to decide the best course of action. The physician also will ask questions about diet, exercise, and social history. Urine and blood samples will be taken and the physician may order extra tests to assess the physical condition of your child. The physician, who will want to monitor weight gain and other signs of recovery as your child restores weight, will also set weight goals and may discuss appropriate levels of activity for your child.

The physician's examination will help show any medical complications of the eating disorder. These involve all body systems. The GI (gastro-intestinal) tract is affected in that many anorectic children suffer from constipation as a result of the slowing down of the digestive tract. This is a result of muscle atrophy and is uncomfortable. Fainting and dizziness are often seen in children with anorexia. This is because of a lowering of blood pressure. Your child's doctor will measure blood pressure in lying, sitting, and standing positions. This not only documents the state of under-nutrition during the first visit, but will also track progress as the numbers improve.

Heart rate is also affected by under-nutrition, and a low heart rate will be carefully monitored by your physician. Your doctor may order an EKG (electrocardiogram) to better asses the condition of your child's heart. If the heart rate is dangerously low your child may be hospitalized for medical stabilization and observation. Although bone density is a serious problem in anorexia, this may not be addressed immediately. This will happen later in treatment. Surprisingly, many of the blood tests of an anorectic are normal, although some specific markers can be in the abnormal range.

Role of the Therapist

The family therapist will help the family with strategies to help parents work against the eating disorder. You will need to meet with the therapist frequently to support the changes needed. The therapist will focus on weight gain and changing eating behavior in the beginning stages of treatment. Later on, the therapist will also help the family identify the ways in which the eating disorder has affected the family. When weight is restored, the support of normal adolescent development becomes the focus of therapy. This process of normal adolescent development can be interrupted when a child develops an eating disorder.

Role of the Nutritionist

The nutritionist will help the family figure out how to meet the calorie needs of a recovering child. However, it is not necessary for anyone to count calories. This takes a lot of time, and your child's weight gain will tell us all we need to know about the caloric adequacy of her diet. The nutritionist will also help the parents identify any family eating patterns that may be detrimental to the recovery process. This book provides many ideas and strategies for this purpose. In many cases, the nutritionist will monitor weight gain as well as provide practical support to the parents. As a child approaches normal weight, the nutritionist can help her relearn normal eating habits. This can take a long time, but it is a very important part of full recovery. This process is discussed in more detail in a later chapter (see "Life After Weight Restoration," page 63).

Confronting the Illness

If you have not even discussed your concerns with your child, then this is the first step. The diagnosis of anorexia nervosa is made when the following criteria are met: 1) a weight of 85% of normal; 2) a distortion of body image (i.e., feeling fat or healthy when in fact the person is very thin); 3) a fear of gaining weight, 4) a low heart rate, and 5) a lack of menstruation in girls.

The signs most obvious to parents of children and adolescents with anorexia nervosa are weight loss, feeling cold all the time, hair loss, and complaints of dizziness, as well as depression and social withdrawal. Preceding these obvious signs are the more subtle ones of a child eating a more healthy diet, a sudden interest in recipes and cooking, avoiding desserts and fried foods, and sometimes a decision to become vegetarian. Other behaviors associated with anorexia are chewing a lot of gum, an increase in the use of salt and spices, and drinking large amounts of diet soda.

If you suspect that your child has an eating disorder it is important to act fast. Not all children will lose weight. Some will stop gaining the weight needed for normal growth. Many children with eating disorders are diagnosed and treated successfully before they are ill enough to meet the criteria for full blown anorexia nervosa. The earlier treatment is started, the better the outcome. Delaying intervention will only strengthen the disorder. When you decide to take action it will mean confronting your child. When doing this it is important to be gentle but firm. Your child cannot have the option of under-eating.

Many parents feel that they are invading their child's autonomy when they try to dictate food choices. Remember: this is an illness. You would not give your sick child a choice of whether or not to take a prescribed medication. Eating disorders can be very serious and are best addressed when they first start. Prompt, gentle, yet firm discussion is the most effective intervention.

There is no denying that this is a difficult conversation to have. Explain what you have noticed. Be specific about what it is you are worried about. This might be a lack of participation in family meals, eating very small amounts of food, excessive exercise, absence of menstruation, and sensitivity to cold as well as weight loss. It might also include other eating disorder behaviors such as cutting food into little pieces, eating alone, eating very slowly, excessive coffee, tea, or diet soda, excessive gum-chewing, and whatever else parents have identified as a new and unhealthy behavior.

Tell your child specifically what you have observed and why this worries you. For example, you might say, "I have noticed that you are often very cold and you have lost weight. This worries me. I would like to make an appointment with your doctor to put my mind at rest."

Most children suffering from anorexia will not be thrilled to get into treatment, but some will be relieved to have help. A book written for caregivers using a family approach to treating eating disorders explains a lot about readiness for change and can help you gauge where your child is on the spectrum of readiness (from very resistant to change to very ready for change). This book makes excellent reading and is called "Skills-based Learning for Caring for a Loved One with an Eating Disorder" by Janet Treasure, Grainne Smith, and Anna Crane. Whether your child is ready for change or not, the goal of the initial stage of family therapy is weight restoration and the interruption of eating disorder behaviors such as skipping family meals or eating very small portions.

The beginning of treatment can be very frightening for your child. It can also be very tiring. The first visit, especially at a coordinated team clinic, can be very long as you may meet with more than one team member. Your child may need to have a variety of laboratory or other tests. Bring snacks, as you may need to eat and not all locations have a cafeteria.

Once your child has been diagnosed, treatment should start right away. If your child is eating a very small amount of food it is wise to start slowly, increasing the amount of food eaten every day for a few days. Start out with small, frequent meals and snacks, about six per day, and slowly increase the quantity. It is not a good idea to suddenly give someone who has been severely restricting their intake a lot of food all at one time. A slow and steady increase is best in the beginning.

When the progression to a more normal amount of food has been accomplished, the real work of weight restoration can begin. This may not go smoothly. During times when the going is tough, remember that you are helping your child confront an eating disorder that has taken hold of her usual thinking about food. A tendency to argue about the contents of a recipe can be avoided by answering with some recognition of the strength of the eating disorder. For example, "Your eating disorder is poking its head into our dinner I see." Keep your voice calm and reassuring even if you are scared inside.

Some universal experiences are shared by parents of children with eating disorders, but not all children will react the same way. For some children the initial eating is very difficult. They are physically bloated and can still be very afraid of certain foods. However, many are remarkably cooperative and feel an immediate sense of relief when they are told that they are no longer in control of their own food choices.

As weight restoration progresses, some of your child's depressed mood may shift to hostility and you may see angry outbursts more frequently for a while. As this is worked through and more weight is restored, you will see a lightening of mood, a lessening of hostility, and a return of the happy child that was lost to the eating disorder. It is important that you don't cave in to their hurt, fear, or hostility. This will only strengthen the eating disorder. Remember, she needs your help to overcome this disorder and to be free to live a normal teenaged life.

In summary

Your child will be best served by a treatment team that consists of a physician, therapist, and nutritionist who are familiar with Maudsley therapy and are able to work together to treat her. Some parents are lucky enough to live close to a team-oriented treatment center. If you are not in this position you can still organize a team for yourself and your child with all the players in place. If you even suspect an eating disorder or the possibility of one, act fast because the sooner this disorder is confronted and treated the easier it will be to treat.

Nutrition in Recovery

You don't really need to know a lot about the science of nutrition to help your child restore weight, but a little information will help make sense of your journey so far and where you are headed.

Effects of Under-Nutrition

To begin, it is useful to know about the experience of 36 physically and psychologically healthy male volunteers who underwent a year-long study on calorie deprivation. The study participants were chosen from a panel of 100 applicants because of their robust physical and psychological health. Dr. Ancel Keys used conscientious objectors to the Second World War to study the effects of starvation. For three months the men ate normally. This was followed by six months of half rations, and then three months of refeeding. Throughout this entire time the men were observed by Dr. Keys and his staff. This allowed the researchers to study in detail the effects of under-nutrition on the men's psychological as well as physical health.

The observations documented in this watershed study, "Biology of Human Starvation," are very familiar to the parents of anorectic children. The men, all healthy and happy to begin with, became universally depressed, irritable, antisocial, and obsessive, especially about food, even during the refeeding phase. Some experienced periods of euphoria followed by a period of depression. Some were so affected psychologically by eating half of their normal food that they were almost psychotic. Remember, these were the healthiest 36 of the 100 who initially volunteered. If you recognize these symptoms in your child, take heart: many of the changes you have seen in your child (depression, antisocial tendencies, obsessional tendencies) will eventually be resolved by weight restoration.

It is important to know that aggressive tendencies in the 36 volunteers increased on refeeding. They were still depressed, just more energetic. Parents in the early stages of weight restoration have seen similar behavior in their children. In the beginning stages of weight restoration, you may have to endure a more aggressive and hostile child who is, of course, still suffering from the food restriction–induced depression. In general, once food intake increases consistently, parents see an improved mood in their child that brings with it a huge sense of relief knowing their beloved child is not permanently changed.

I would like to share a quote by Laura Collins author of "Eating with Your Anorexic" (see Books, page 187).

> "Parents need—and deserve—to know that the tantrums, thrown food, and extreme behaviors of early recovery are not unusual. There is no easy, quick, simple, or painless way out of an eating disorder. No matter how compliant and easy your child has always been, plan for extreme reactions and decide in advance what you will do to keep yourself and your family safe

and calm. The distress isn't easier in a hospital or inpatient facility or a residential center, though it may be more internal and out of sight."

It is important to know that your child's eating disorder is not going to give up without a fight, and you will have to dig deep and be strong to fight back.

The physiological effects of under-nutrition are many. One organ very affected by an eating disorder is the brain. The brain functions by using glucose. The source of glucose in the diet is carbohydrates. When a child severely restricts carbohydrates, this will affect her brain function in ways that you have noticed, such as depressed mood and an inability to concentrate. Your child's inability to concentrate, as well as some of the mood issues, will be resolved by persuading her to eat carbohydrates such as bread, crackers, pasta, rice, fruit, cereal, corn, beans, potatoes, etc. Similarly, the body needs fat for hormone production. Any delay in your child's physical maturation will start to be corrected with the reintroduction of fat into the diet and as your child restores weight.

Children with eating disorders are often very afraid of eating fat. They have many misconceptions about how much and what type of fat they should eat. In general, the type of fat is less important for your purposes than the amount. Expect them to argue about the pros and cons of different types of fat. For a child who is eating about 3,000 calories, the American Heart Association recommends 100 grams of fat daily. (There is no need for you or your child to count fat grams; this information is provided only to put the fat content of a food as written on the nutrition label in perspective.) Even a high-fat food will not go much above 15 grams of fat per serving, which is low compared with the amount recommended by the American Heart Association.

It is important to know that the basal metabolic rate (BMR) of a person who has been underfed is lowered by at least 30% and possibly 40%. When you start to restore your child's weight her metabolic rate will increase. So despite an increase in the amount of food your child is eating, the weight gain may be small because of an increase in metabolic rate to as high as 120% or even 130% of normal as your child rebuilds tissues. This is why recovering children can need to eat anywhere from 3,000 to 4,000 calories a day.

Remember: do not count calories. It is not necessary and it is exhausting. I know the calorie, protein, fat, and carbohydrate content of the recipes in this book. If you needed to know this and work with the numbers to help your child get better, then I would have included them. Use your child's increasing weight as the measure of your success. Counting calories will be distracting and time-consuming. Your energy is better spent persuading your child to eat more than they are comfortable with or even relaxing and taking care of yourself!

Gaining weight is a lot of work for your child and requires a phenomenal amount of food. To ensure the required calories, your child cannot skimp on breakfast or lunch and will need to eat three snacks (mid-morning, mid-afternoon, and evening). Drinks such as milk or juice, when consumed with meals and snacks, also will help. A high-calorie drink can be substituted for a snack any time your child feels overwhelmed by the quantity of food that needs to be eaten every day. (There are more details on this in the the chapter "Meal Planning," page 45.)

More tips: Your child will complain of fullness, and will feel very bloated after meals. Although this is typical, it is still uncomfortable. Foods dense in calories will help to keep the volume of food, and the feeling of an overstretched stomach, down. If bloating occurs, a heating pad on your child's stomach might be helpful. Passage of time and more normal eating are the only things that will remedy this discomfort.

If gas is a problem, try substituting Lactaid milk to see if this helps. Sometimes, but not always, recovering patients are temporarily lactose-intolerant. Lactaid milk has been altered to remove the lactose, which is a naturally occurring sugar in regular milk. It is normally digested by gut enzymes. However, when the gut has been underfed for a while, enzyme levels sometimes can be temporarily reduced. If this happens, the lactose will be digested by gut bacteria, causing gas. This is a temporary situation. As your child's gut returns to normal, so will the level of gut enzymes that digest lactose. Yogurt contains less lactose than milk and should be more easily tolerated if lactose intolerance is a problem. Cheese is lactose-free and will be tolerated well.

Constipation is a chronic problem with recovering children. It may take awhile before this is resolved. This may be one of the most disruptive consequences of under-nutrition in the immediate weight restoration phase, as children often have a hard time eating to over-fullness when they feel bloated because of constipation. The gut of a recovering child is very slow because the muscular contractions that propel food along the digestive tract (called peristalsis) are not as strong. Regular food and weight restoration will correct this over time. Here are some ideas that might lessen the intensity of the problem while you wait for the gut to recover.

I have found that patients who eat a lot of dried fruit and nuts seem to have an easier time with this problem. Dried prunes (about three a day, every day) can help, too. I had one patient who solved the problem by drinking an 8-ounce glass of mixed prune and cranberry juice every day. Fruits and vegetables help too, as do high-fiber cereals (look for more than 5 grams of fiber per serving). I advise patients to drink about 32 ounces of water (the amount in two water bottles) daily between meals. (But still serve juice or milk with meals).

Although I recommend water and fruit to prevent consti-pation, it is important not to let your child fill up on these. Some children with eating disorders get in the habit of drinking lots of water before and during a meal to add to the feeling of fullness. Some children can eat lots of fruits and vegetables to feel full. While fruits and vegetables are very healthy, they don't add a lot of calories, but they do contribute a lot to fullness. So, although you definitely want vegetables in your child's diet, be careful about the quantities you serve because they are filling without adding a lot of calories to the meal. Many patients have also used over-the-counter fiber supplements.

Research has shown the benefits of probiotics in the treatment of GI disorders, including constipation. Probiotics work by repopulating the gut with bacteria normally found in the intestine that help with digestion. The normal micro flora in the gut of anorectic children may have been disrupted because of their limited choice of foods. There has been no research on the effect of probiotics on the constipation associated with anorexia nervosa, but in case it helps (and it won't do any harm) I recommend yogurts that contain live bacteria for my patients. The best choice currently is Stonyfield yogurt, as it has the widest variety of types of bacteria. Try to buy the cartons with the longest time to expiration because they will have a higher concentration of the bacteria. Two 8-ounce cartons per day would be a good amount, but if you can only get your child to eat one, that is better than none. There are also over-the-counter supplements available at pharmacies that you could use instead of yogurt. Ask at your local pharmacy for a supplement with the widest variety of intestinal bacteria. It can take up to six weeks of daily consumption of a probiotic for any improvement to be seen.

One of the most serious problems with chronically underweight children is the loss of bone density. Some children, if left untreated, can even have osteoporosis. For a girl, bone rebuilding will not start until her weight is restored and she has resumed normal, regular menstruation. Oral contraceptives, although they regulate the menstrual cycle, do not help with bone density. Weight gain and adequate calories are what is needed. Once restored to a healthy body weight, children will begin depositing calcium in their bones.

Once this happens, make sure your child has 3–4 servings of milk or milk products per day as well as a calcium and vitamin D supplement. Most supplements contain about 500–600 mg of calcium. A glass of milk has about 300 mg, which is the amount in one and a half ounces of cheese or a cup of yogurt. Cottage cheese and cream cheese are not good sources of calcium, although cottage cheese is a good source of protein. Soy milk is usually fortified with calcium and vitamin D. The calcium can settle on the bottom of the carton, so make sure that the carton gets a good shake before use. Other foods also contain calcium, such as some leafy green vegetables, but the calcium in those foods is not well absorbed. For this reason, if your child does not eat dairy products, you will need to use supplements. I recommend about 1,500 mg of calcium per day after weight is restored to normal.

What To Do About "Fear Foods"

Your child has, I am sure, many foods they have stopped eating. These are usually foods they are afraid to eat because they are high in fat or carbohydrate. They often include butter, cheese, mayonnaise as well as bread, pasta and rice. Some children are afraid to fear foods believing, that if they start to eat them they will not be able to stop. Most children object to a particular macronutrient (usually either carbohydrate or fat) in the food and believe that this macronutrient is harmful when eaten. Different children have different scary foods. These fears need to be conquered for full recovery. Many children regain their lost weight but are not persuaded to conquer their disordered thinking about "good vs. bad" foods. They remain at risk for relapse until they are able to eat all foods.

There are several different strategies for helping children conquer their fear foods. Some parents jump in the deep end, increasing calories and introducing fear foods at the same time. Other parents start out increasing the quantity of safe foods and then slowly start introducing "scary" foods, perhaps at a rate of one per week. You will need to decide how to deal with this issue, what will work for your family and for your particular child. If your child is reluctant you will have a fight on your hands no matter which strategy you decide to use. Those parents who start slowly will not give recipes like those in this book at the beginning, instead they give simpler, less threatening dishes to start. They will use higher calorie recipes when their child becomes more cooperative. Others parents use these high calorie options from the very beginning and endure the battles that may rage.

Gentle persuasion, not logical discussion is what is needed here. Saying something like "being afraid of cheese is a part of your eating disorder" will be more effective than saying something like "cheese is healthy and is a good source of protein and calcium". Getting into a discussion of the pros and cons of cheese will not be as effective as working against the behavior of avoiding cheese.

However, once these foods are introduced, it is important that your child continues to eat these "scary" foods on a regular basis for a while. This will help get the food into a more neutral place in your child's mind. Children who have a broader range of food choices at their return to normal weight seem to do better long-term. Research results show that the adolescents who eat foods with a higher density of calories (think fried breaded chicken instead of grilled chicken) and those with a wider variety of food choices during recovery have much less chance of having the eating disorder return. It is because of this that I stress the importance of confronting food fears during the recovery period. Even with a full weight restoration, if your child continues to have food fears the eating disorder is not beaten. You may be able to identify foods that fit into your child's fear food list. Knowing this will help you figure out a plan for helping your child overcome these fears.

Your child is not better until she can eat pizza, chocolate, ice cream, cookies, French fries, cheeseburgers, and other foods of this type and enjoy them without any hesitation or anxiety. The expectation is not that your child will eat these foods every day and that is not the point – the point is that when your child does eat these foods that they are relaxed enough about the foods to really enjoy them. The scary food will need to be given over and over until it becomes neutral. It might take up to 8 times for this to happen but don't give up because it is so important to permanent recovery

How To Talk to an Eating Disorder

Many parents with anorectic children talk about the effects of ED (Eating Disorder) on their child's thinking. It will be impossible to reason with your child while the eating disorder's grip is very strong. In a malnourished state your child will not be able to think logically. It is not until she is more recovered and at a normal weight that you will be able to talk scientifically about food with her. During the difficult meals you will need to stay calm and reassuring, you should not try to use logic or your fears for her long term health to persuade her to eat. To best help your child, focus your energy on challenging the disordered behaviors. You will need to challenge the eating disorder thoughts at a later time. You will need to develop skills in persuading your child to eat one mouthful more than they can comfortably do each time they eat. Below are some examples of how you might be able to talk to your child when feeding her results in conflict. Although the task ahead can seem formidable, children do recover.

Examples of What Not To Say

Examples of What To Say

That is not enough food for a baby – what do you mean you are full?

I know it is hard but you have to have courage to stand up to the eating disorder.

I can't believe you are not eating it all – you promised!

I know you can do it – I am here to support you.

It's not that high in fat – it said on the label it only had 10 grams.

I don't want to discuss nutrition details with you now – I just want you to eat more.

In summary

Under-nutrition takes its toll on your child's physical and psychological health. These range from insufficient fat to make hormones for growth to depression and anxiety. As your child eats her basal metabolic rate will increase as will her appetite. She may suffer uncomfortable symptoms as her gastro-intestinal tract recovers. It is important to make sure that she eats not only enough food to recover but a wide variety of foods especially those high in calories for long term recovery. In persuading your child to eat using logic will be futile. You will need to be loving but firm, reminding her that your job is to help her fight the eating disorder.

I am not afraid of storms,
for I am learning how
to sail my ship.

Louisa May Alcott

Family Food Culture

This chapter explores the eating style of your family. Family food culture is essentially how your family relates to food and the feeding of family members. While your child is recovering from an eating disorder the family culture around food is important. There are several components to how your family handles food and meals. One important aspect is the family history regarding the division of responsibility in feeding children; another is the central meal planning system in the house. A key factor in family food culture is the parents' attitude and habits regarding food and weight.

Division of responsibility

It is important to point out that restoring weight in a child with anorexia breaks the usually recommended division of responsibility in feeding children in a family. I think it is worth spelling out exactly what the difference is. Although many parents grew up in families where children were expected to clean their plates, the division of responsibility, (as described by Ellen Satter in her book "Child of Mine") between parents and children is recommended to be as follows:

You the parent, decide where, when, and pretty much what your family eats. The child is in control of how much. You are used to being able to trust your child to eat enough to fill them. Children are presented with food at appropriate times and encouraged to eat a balanced meal. The following table shows this very important division of responsibility.

Division of responsibility feeding children without an eating disorder

Parent	Child
What	How much
Where	
When	

This is how feeding works best under normal circumstances. As parents, you make rules about where food can be eaten: in the kitchen, not in the bedrooms; or whatever your particular restrictions are. You also choose mealtimes. Usually, you the parent, decide what food will be purchased and cooked, and therefore what the family will eat. This is how feeding children works best and is probably what has worked for you in the past.

The division of responsibility starts to blur a bit with teenagers as they start to assume more responsibility for some of these decisions, often deciding when, where, what, and always how much they want to eat. Now, to facilitate your child's recovery, you are faced with having to break the current recommended division of responsibility. This is why taking back control from your child for all aspects of feeding may not seem right or fair. Not only are you moving her back to a younger feeding relationship, but you are taking more control than you had even when she was younger. The table below illustrates the feeding relationship with the eating-disordered child.

Division of responsibility feeding children with an eating disorder

Parent	Child
What	
Where	Eat what your parents
When	give you to eat.
How much	

I have heard parents say that it seems disrespectful of their child's independence to do this. However, the change is only in regard to food. Parents are also afraid that because eating disorders often have been associated with a "good" child's search for control that this recommendation might make matters worse. The data shows the opposite: Children who are fed at home and are made to relinquish control of self-feeding do better and recover more quickly than children who are left in control of their own food while they see an individual psychotherapist.

Remember, your child can stay independent in other areas of her life. To make progress, you now will need to redefine the division of responsibility of feeding to accomplish your goals. You will not only need to retake control of what, where, and when your child eats, but now you also have to add something that you have not really ever tried to control before: you have to decide how much.

You have to imagine that your child is "portion blind." She has temporarily lost the ability to judge the amount of food she should

...it is up to you to help her receive and eat a healthy and appropriate amount of food. Your job is to reassure your child that you will take control of this, and that she can trust you to make sure she will eat the right amount of food for her body.

Many patients admit they are afraid to start eating because they think they will not be able to stop. Some do feel a sense of relief when they are persuaded to hand over the control of food portions to their parents. Others can be reluctant to do so at the beginning. However, over time the sense of relief is almost universal. One of the aspects of this disorder is that as a child's body weight decreases, the urge to compensate by overeating can become very powerful. The only way she has been able to deny her physiological urge to eat a lot of food is to exert more and more control over the amount and types of food eaten.

This fear of overeating is physiologically based and in the past, patients have sometimes progressed from anorexia nervosa to binge eating and bulimia. Maudsley therapy reduces the chance that these other eating disorders will be a part of the outcome of your child's anorexia nervosa. Because this fear is real, I believe it is fair to promise your child that you will monitor her eating to prevent overeating once she has regained a healthy body weight. We also always reassure our patients that we will not let them become overweight, and that we have a plan for them after they have restored their weight to a healthy place. (For more information on this, see "Life After Weight Restoration," page 63.)

Meal organization

Children and adolescents with eating disorders have often become very involved in the food choices of the family. This can be through cooking, baking, or shopping. Many children will benefit from not being involved in any aspect of meal preparation until they are recovered. Not being in the kitchen at all during cooking may be a good idea for them. You will need to judge how this works for your family. Some families find a middle ground where the child, while not involved in any meal preparation, can still bake cookies, bread, or whatever else she enjoys.

I recommend that meal planning and recipe selection should be done without your child. When I counsel parents, I usually meet with them alone, especially at the beginning. This is to reinforce the fact that a child with anorexia nervosa is not in control of food choices for the time being. It is better to free them from any thoughts about what the family should eat, including what recipes you may choose from this book.

During the weight restoration phase of recovery, there should be a lot of organization around the planning and preparation of food. One contributor to a family's food culture is the frequency of family meals. With current lifestyles of two working parents and busy extracurricular activities, food planning and preparation can sometimes become less of a priority. Detailed meal planning will reduce the daily stress of cooking. Many families find it a good idea to have a weekly menu plan that is decided on and shopped for over the weekend. In the next chapter I explore general meal planning ideas to try to reduce stress. I also have ideas for each meal to maximize calories.

Family attitude to dieting, weight, and food

The relationship the parents themselves have with food also

influences the family's attitude to food. Some parents are "intuitive eaters," while others are dieting or have other food-related issues. Some parents are simply trying to lose a few pounds, while others can have eating disorders themselves and be prone to binging, excessive exercise, or self-induced vomiting. Some families have a culture of being critical of the weight and body shape of other people (even TV characters). Parents can also be over-invested in their child's weight or shape.

Families sometimes categorize foods into "good" and "bad." They may feel guilty when "bad" foods are consumed and virtuous when "good" foods are eaten. Foods such as pizza, ice cream, and cookies might be eaten guiltily and seen as unhealthy, or be eaten only as a deserved treat.

It is important that you, as parents, really understand your own relationship with food as you help your child recover. Although eating healthy food is the goal of most families, some families are overzealous in this pursuit. These parents eat only those foods they see as nutritious and never have empty-calorie foods. Children need to see their parents eating and enjoying all kinds of food. I often tell my patients that although there are no "bad" foods, there can be bad diets. The message your child needs to hear loud and clear is that it is all a matter of balance and that all foods can be eaten in the context of a healthy diet.

Because your child has an eating disorder, your house will need to become a neutral place in terms of food. All food must be welcome and eaten. Body acceptance needs to be modeled by both parents. If you must be on a diet for health reasons, it will be best not to discuss this with your child in order to minimize the possible triggering effect your diet might have on her behavior. Do not discuss your body, your child's body, or anyone else's body. It is also a good idea to get rid of fashion magazines as these can be triggering because of their focus on body image.

Let me emphasize that there is no data to suggest that dieting parents cause eating disorders, and that it is not the intent of this section to lay blame or cause any parental guilt over prior eating habits. There are many people on diets and with various attitudes about food whose children do not have eating disorders. However, your child has shown vulnerability in this area, perhaps because of a genetic predisposition to anorexia nervosa.

To help with recovery and to prevent relapse, your child's home environment will need to be food-neutral. In the section "Life After Weight Restoration" (page 63), I describe "intuitive eating." This is a pattern of eating that will protect your child from eating disorders in the future. If you need some help working toward this yourself you might want to read ahead. Your child will not be ready for any of the information in this chapter until her weight is restored. If you have a history of dieting, you may find the information especially useful in setting up a food-neutral home.

In summary

To best facilitate recovery, parents must change the normal division of control in feeding their child. They must now take over control of how much, as well as when, what, and where their child eats. Organized family meal planning and preparation will lessen the stress around mealtimes and help in recovery because of this. Parents must make their homes food-neutral, which means that it will have no dieting, no comments on body size, and a policy that all foods are welcome.

✧✧

Courage is like a muscle.

We strengthen it with use.

Ruth Gordan

✧✧

Meal Planning

Meal planning has been lost in the daily business of many families. Many parents stand peering into their refrigerator hoping for inspiration at the end of a busy day. In the home of a child with an eating disorder this can be disastrous. Mealtimes with an anorectic child at the table are usually very stressful. I have found that families really benefit from organized food production. Plan menus on the weekend with detailed grocery lists so all needed foods are purchased in one trip, avoiding multiple last-minute trips to the grocery store.

Set goals you know you can achieve in terms of organization. This may mean a simple but high-calorie breakfast, and a lunch that requires only last-minute preparation (as is the case with a sandwich, juice, and fruit). Dinner may be a time to be more creative. Some meals can be cooked ahead of time and stored, and many high-calorie prepared dishes are available in the freezer section of your grocery store. These come with nutrition labels, which can present a problem since many children with eating disorders cannot eat a food without looking at the nutrition label if one is available.

Just remember: planning is the key. Whether you buy or

make the high-calorie food your child needs is less important. Planning will prove its worth as the day-to-day stress of cooking is reduced and a family culture of organized, planned food preparation becomes the norm.

Breakfast

Much research has shown the benefits – for all children – of eating a balanced meal at breakfast time. These include higher intakes of vitamins and minerals, less distractibility, and better weight control. Despite this, breakfast is a meal that is often overlooked when everyone is in a rush in the morning. It is important for everyone in the family to eat breakfast, but for children needing to consume enough calories for weight restoration it is essential. A good breakfast, calorie-wise, will take pressure off the meals eaten later in the day and will start the day off in a nonrestrictive way. When breakfast is small, other meals will need to be larger to meet your child's significant calorie needs.

The trick is to condense calories here because everyone is in a hurry. Breakfast for your child can be as simple as a one high-calorie food and one high-calorie drink. The section Breakfast Recipes (page 77) has lots of high-calorie recipes to prepare on the weekend or on a free evening. Many use canola oil because it is high in omega-3 fats. I have also added ground flaxseed as an optional ingredient to many recipes. This can be purchased in whole food stores and is available over the Internet. Once ground, it must be stored in the refrigerator since the fat in flaxseed goes rancid quickly at room temperature.

Here are some ideas for breakfast:

- Muffins, store-bought (any kind except low-fat) with a high-calorie drink such as the hot chocolate recipe on page 106; any of the drinks in the Drinks Recipes section (page 106) would be a good complement to the muffin.

- Bagels with peanut butter or cream cheese and juice.

- Scone with butter or jam and a high-calorie drink (Drinks Recipes, page 106).

- Granola with fruit and juice. The granola in Breakfast Recipes (page 77) is quite high in calories, and being homemade it has no nutrition label.

- A baked breakfast (recipes on pages 80 – 82), plus a fruit smoothie (recipe on page 109). Bake the breakfast the night before and just microwave it in the morning to save time and early morning hassle.

The routine of eating the same food every day for breakfast is reassuring for some children. This can work as long as there is some exposure to fear foods during the day. You will need to work out what works best for your family. You may decide to start each day with the agenda of risk-taking; or you may decide that the stress of the morning rush to school precludes presenting new risk food during breakfast. Either way, I hope the ideas in this section help with this important meal.(Recipes for breakfast foods start on page 77).

Lunch

Lunch is a meal that is important to structure in such a way as to maximize calories. It is still early in the day and is a meal that can also be "routine." As with breakfast, recovering children often do well with repetition.

If your child is attending school, she will find many challenges associated with this meal. The timing of lunch can vary a lot from school to school, even semester to semester, but it can be as early as 10:30 a.m. The time allowed for eating lunch can be from 20 to 30 minutes. This can be a difficult period for your child, especially if it takes her a long time to get through her food. So again, caloric density is important to ensure that enough calories can be consumed in such a short time.

Your child may have been packing her own lunch or even insisting on buying it, therefore keeping you out of the loop. This will have to be reevaluated in the weight restoration phase of recovery. In the beginning stages of recovery, you should select the foods and pack them yourself. You will need to send your child to school with a lunch that you feel meets her needs. Choosing foods at lunch from the cafeteria menu may trigger eating disorder thoughts that she then must overcome to make the appropriate choice. It is better not to give the eating disorder a chance to influence her in this way. This is why I recommend packing a lunch in the beginning stages of recovery.

It is important to think about ways to ensure that your child actually is eating the food you send. Many parents will eat lunch with their child at school to make sure they are eating. In some schools eating lunch in the nurse's office, under supervision, is an option. You will need to decide if this is necessary. If your child is gaining weight at a good rate and you are not supervising school lunches then you may not need to do either. However, if the rate of gain is not good, you may want to consider eating lunch with her, or having a nurse or other staff member supervise the lunchtime meal if the school has the resources for this.

It may not be possible to get your child to eat all this food in the first few weeks of recovery. In the beginning stage you will just be doing the best you can to get your child to eat one more spoonful than they are comfortable with. However, when your child is eating well and restoring weight, try out the ideas and the recipes in the Lunch Recipes section (page 61). These ideas are not better than your own choices but they may get you thinking along the right track in this important stage of recovery.

Suggestions for what to pack

- **Sandwich.** This is always a good idea. Try a triple-decker: three slices of bread with filling. Turkey is a good source of protein and is usually acceptable to children with eating disorders, but it is low in calories. You will need to put at least three slices in a sandwich. Because of turkey's low fat content, it is better to push a slice of cheese than an extra slice of turkey. Tuna salad and chicken salad are great because they have mayonnaise, providing much-needed fat. I have included some sandwich ideas later in this section.

- **Wraps.** These can be a nice alternative to sandwiches and sometimes are more acceptable and easier to use at the beginning. A wrap has a fairly large surface area and is great for using spreads: hummus, pesto, guacamole, olives, and cream cheese. Any dip can be used as a spread. The Lunch Recipes section (page 61) contains a spread made from beans and cream cheese. There are recipes for other dips and spreads in the Snack Recipes section (page 96).

- **Juice or milk**. Send your child to school with one of these, or have her buy them at school. Some families serve milk or juice with meals and snacks and water between meals. Children often find that a can of Ensure or Boost with lunch takes some of the eating pressure off, especially in the early stages.

- **Fruit.** Pack a fruit as well. Bananas, grapes, dried fruit, and applesauce are all excellent choices as they have more calories than berries or vegetables.

- **Trail mix.** This is also an excellent addition to your child's lunch because it is high in both calories and fiber. It may also be seen as healthy, and thus more acceptable than potato chips. Interestingly tortilla chips may be seen as less scary than potato chips, so they may be a good place to start.

- **Cookies.** As soon as possible, start adding cookies to your child's lunch. These foods may be on a "forbidden" list, but these fears will need to be confronted for full recovery. Sometimes a Fig Newton–type cookie is a little less scary than a chocolate chip type, but progress must to be made to include all types of cookies.

Two lunch examples:

- Tuna salad sandwich, juice box, banana, tortilla chips, cookie

- Avocado, turkey, and cheese wrap, trail mix, milk (2%

or whole), granola bar

Below are additional ideas for sandwiches and wraps. Recipes for other lunch foods are in the Lunch Recipes section starting on page 61.

Sandwiches and Wraps

(*vegetarian; ** vegan)

Peanut or almond butter and jelly**

Nut butter sandwiches on small crackers**

Hummus (or other spread), shredded carrots, and celery rolled in a wrap**

Hummus and diced olives on whole wheat bread**

Pesto bean dip (page 94), sliced olives, and goat cheese in a wrap**

Cannellini bean spread (page 94) with roasted vegetables in a wrap**

Leftover pasta or grain dishes in a wrap**

Pesto and roasted vegetables in a wrap**

Pesto, cheese and roasted vegetables in a wrap*

Cucumbers or tomatoes and cream cheese with sprouts in a wrap*

Cream cheese and jelly sandwiches, cut into quarters or fingers*

Avocado, turkey, and cheese, sandwich or wrap

Beans and roasted vegetables in a wrap**

Hummus in a pita pocket with roasted vegetables**

Avocado and roasted vegetables in a pita pocket**

Ham-and-cheese sandwich

Grilled cheese

Hummus in a pita pocket with bean salad**

Sliced avocado and cheese in a pita pocket*

Cold tofu burger, pesto, and avocado on a whole wheat bun**

Two mini-bagels with pesto, lunch meat, cheese, and lettuce

Snacks

Snacks are very important in weight restoration. The caloric demands of recovery can be very high and are hard to satisfy in only three meals. Many children protest that eating frequently during the day is harder than eating three large meals. But with the problems of early fullness and bloating that come with weight restoration, it is hard for a child to consume what they need eating only breakfast, lunch, and dinner.

Many families have set up a schedule of three meals and three snacks during the initial weight restoration phase. Others have managed to restore their child's weight without the mid-morning snack. This can be a problem if the child is continuing at school during recovery, especially if lunch time is very early. Other families make arrangements with the school to have a snack given during the morning in the nurse's office. Again, you will need to decide what will work for your child and your family.

If you decide to give a mid-morning snack at school, pre-packed snacks (in ziplock bags) can be left in the school nurse's office to be eaten there at set times. For example, a bag with a juice box and graham crackers with peanut butter could be left there to be eaten at 9 a.m. With time, a variety of snacks can be left and your child can start choosing which ones to eat. You will need to decide when your child is ready to make this transition. It will depend on how well she is doing and whether you feel that she is ready to start having some control over any food choice. In my experience, this happens when a child approaches an ideal body weight and some of the rigidity around food lessens.

Your child should eat a snack soon after arriving home from school. If this snack is delayed until too close to dinner, that meal will be difficult.

A snack while studying or before going to bed is a good approach to encourage the evening snack. Some children do well with a high-calorie drink (see Drinks Recipes, page 106) and not a lot of food at this point, as they can be tired from the day's eating, which is so much work for them. A bowl of ice cream can also be an easy snack unless lactose intolerance is a problem. Ice cream is a food that will frequently be on the fear food list and will also need to be challenged during recovery.

Providing a drink with calories (milk or juice) with snacks can boost energy intake without contributing to fullness. I have included a chapter on high-calorie drinks, which can substitute for a snack if desired. Sometimes drinking calories can be easier than eating, but many patients have a hard time drinking anything except water at the beginning of recovery. This behavior belongs in the fear food category and will need to be challenged if your child is to fully recover.

You will be able to figure out the best plan for your child. I strongly recommend "front loading," that is, trying to get as many calories in as possible at the beginning of the day. If you do not manage to do this, you may see an increase in family stress as you try to push food at the end of the day when everyone is tired.

Many foods can be used at snack time: regular yogurt, applesauce, crackers with peanut butter, puddings with whipped cream, bagel with cream cheese, and store-bought muffins. Granola bars are sometimes a "neutral food" to a child with an eating disorder. Better granola-type bars are cereal bars, which you will find in the breakfast cereal aisle. Energy or sports bars are even higher in calories and protein than typical granola bars or cereal bars. They are usually located in the health food section of grocery stores, in pharmacies, and in some whole food stores. These bars will vary a lot from brand to brand; check the labels to help decide which ones to buy.

Quick Snack Ideas

The following snacks are reasonable choices for a child in recovery. The portions are meant only as a rough guide. Neither you nor your child should measure any food served.

Milk or juice
English muffin with butter
2 slices of cheese

1 apple

Peanut butter
Milk or juice

Milk or juice
6–8 saltine crackers with peanut butter

1 cup yogurt
½ cup granola
Milk or juice

Cereal with milk
Juice
Banana or 1 cup of berries

½ bagel with 1 tablespoon peanut butter
Milk or juice

4 fig bars
Milk
4 Chips Ahoy cookies
Milk

1 yogurt (regular)
1 piece of fruit

Sports bar
Milk or juice

2 granola bars
Milk or juice

The Snack Recipes section (page 96) has recipes for homemade granola bars, sweetbreads, dips and spreads which can be used for more snack ideas.

Drinks

Many patients in recovery will use some sort of liquid supplement, whether homemade or purchased, during the weight restoration phase. Gaining weight is a lot of work, especially when the metabolic rate is revved up. These drinks can relieve some of the pressure to eat what can seem like a large amount of food.

A substantial drink with breakfast is a great way to increase calories. Sometimes people use drinks as a snack substitute when a child seems overwhelmed.

There are very good ready-to-use drinks available both in stores and online. The smoothies at coffee outlets are usually the highest in calories, followed by lattes and then "Coolata" type drinks, especially if made with cream. The flavored milk section in grocery stores has undergone a complete makeover in recent years and there are many good choices there. Even some diet shakes traditionally used as meal replacements can make a good contribution if used as part of a snack. But they cannot be used as meal replacements in this situation.

In the Drinks Recipes section (page 106) I have listed recipes for high-calorie drinks. Most have some milk or other dairy choice but some are milk-free. If lactose intolerance is a problem you can substitute Lactaid milk, vanilla yogurt, or soy milk for the milk in the recipes. Half-and-half is also an option for an even higher-calorie drink. Some of the recipes are very simple (the hot chocolate recipe, for example) and some are more complicated.

Ready-to-use supplemental drinks:

Ensure Plus, 8-ounce
Resource Plus
Boost Plus
Carnation Instant Breakfast
Milk shake from fast-food restaurant
Slim•Fast
Yogurt smoothies
Flavored milks

Dinner

Many children find dinner the most difficult meal of the day. There are many reasons for this. Dinner is the meal with the most variety. The routine of the same foods for breakfast and lunch, if comforting for your child, cannot be continued at dinner. It is not normal for families to eat the same food for dinner every night. Dinner is often the largest meal of the day for many families, and it is usually the most social. Families frequently eat out for dinner and many celebrations occur at dinnertime, all of which can cause anxiety for a child with anorexia nervosa.

A family dinner can be very stressful because trying to carry on a normal conversation when one of the people at the table has an eating disorder is very difficult. The whole family is affected by this. If normal conversation is not possible, adding a structured type of conversation will provide a distraction from disordered thinking about food for your recovering child. It will also give your other children relief from mealtime tension. Many parents have come up with clever ways to lighten dinnertime interactions. One is to have the parents take turns reading aloud from a book that is continued from one evening to the next.

Another is to read though Trivial Pursuit questions or other game cards. One family watched reruns of a favorite TV show.

With dinner, as with other meals, the idea is to use recipes that are high in calories. In this way, the volume of food that needs to be eaten is more manageable than trying to use food less dense in energy. Examples of the kinds of food to serve include lasagna, chicken pot pie, mashed potatoes, risotto, casseroles with cream sauces, recipes with hamburger meat, etc.

The Dinner Recipes section (pages 111 - 170) contains many recipes that are high in calories. I have added many side dishes that complement a meal with a lower-calorie entrée. It is not necessary to have a high-calorie entrée and a high-calorie side dish, especially if you have been able to get in the habit of high-calorie breakfasts and lunches. Again, a steady weight gain will let you know if you are succeeding in feeding your child enough calories.

The Dinner Recipes section contains recipes for various pasta sauces (starting on page 168). Many of these, such as pesto and Alfredo sauce, can be purchased ready-made in stores. For marinara sauce, be sure to add grated cheese, olives, and maybe a little extra olive oil to boost calories.

High-calorie sauces served over grilled meats will add calories and could be omitted for those family members who need a lower-calorie dinner. There are sauce recipes in the Dinner Recipes section (starting on page 168). These two recipes from the Dips and Spreads section can also be used as sauces: Guacamole (page 103) and Feta Walnut Dip (page103).

Serving grilled meat with a heavy side dish is another option for families with a member who needs a lower-calorie or lower-fat menu for medical or other reasons. They can either not eat or eat just a very small portion of the side. Side Dish recipes start on page 153.

The baked Breakfast Recipes (starting on page 79) also can be used as a dinner entrée and served with a hearty side dish or salad.

As I have said before, the recipes I have included are only examples for you to use. Take a look at your family recipes and I am sure you will find that many are high in calories and can meet the needs of your child during the weight restoration phase.

Desserts

The foods in the Desserts Recipes chapter (page 178) are usually in the category of fear foods. I have included some uncommon recipes, as well as some familiar ones. You will need to decide if the usual or unusual will be the least difficult your child, though I expect that neither will be easy.

Some children do not react as we expect (that is, with anger and resistance). Some are ready for help and feel relief at not having to battle along on their own. Once they start to broaden their food choices they really enjoy the previously forbidden food during the weight restoration phase. For some children, this will end their fear of these foods and they will start to enjoy them as any teenager would. Other children can allow these foods while they are restoring weight, but the foods are still not neutral for them. They may start to show some resistance to eating them as they approach a healthy weight. You will need to persuade your child to eat these foods until they become neutral.

Let me say again, that it is important for your child to have no forbidden foods by the end stage of treatment. I do not expect that your child will eat fear foods at every meal. However, she needs to be able to eat any dessert and believe it is okay to have a dessert at least two or three times per week – and it really is. Sometimes it can work better to go out for ice cream or dessert on a weekly basis. This will depend on your child. You will have to make the decision as to the best foods to introduce and where and when to do it.

Vegetarianism and Eating Disorders

Many children with eating disorders become vegetarian during the course of the disorder. I think it is very important to question your child's decision to become vegetarian when you are helping her recover. Is it really based on beliefs about the use of animals for food? Sometimes a decision to become vegetarian is actually a decision prompted by the eating disorder as a way to restrict certain fear foods. It is up to you to decide which is the case with your child.

A vegetarian diet can be adequate in calories, fat, and protein if the right foods are chosen. Cheese and eggs are great choices for vegetarians because they are excellent sources of protein. The thing to remember with vegetable sources of protein is that the quantity needed to meet protein requirements is substantial and often difficult for a child with anorexia. For example, it takes 1½ cups of beans or tofu to provide the same amount of protein as a small chicken breast. This quantity of beans or tofu may seem overwhelming to a recovering child. Beans with cheese mixed in can decrease the volume of food. Three quarters of a cup of beans with two ounces of shredded cheese has the same amount of protein as 1½ cups of beans with half the volume. Meat substitute products can vary a lot in protein content. Anything with 18 or more grams of protein per serving is a good source.

Most vegetarians will eat dairy products and eggs. However, some, known as vegans, are much stricter and will eat no animal products at all including butter, cheese, or even foods made with gelatin. It is very difficult to select foods with enough fat and protein in a vegan diet. For recovery to take place, I would recommend serving eggs and dairy products and expecting your child to eat them until she is recovered. She can always resume a vegan diet when you feel she is fully recovered.

If your whole family is vegan, you must ensure that your child is eating a source of protein and soy milk with every meal and snack. I would also recommend conscious fat inclusion in the form of oils (canola), salad dressings, lots of nuts, and nut butters, as well as hummus, avocado, olives, and margarine. Children following a vegan diet will also need a supplemental source of vitamin B12.

For all children, vegetarian or not, coconut milk is an excellent source of fat and calories and may be more acceptable than other foods since it is not usually on the fear foods list.

Helpful ideas for parents of vegetarian children also are available in other sections of this book. For example, many of the pasta and side dish recipes are vegetarian. I have also included ideas for vegetarian lunches in the Lunch Recipes section.

Life After Weight Restoration

As time has passed, you have experienced the joy of seeing your child's weight restored to a healthy place. You also will have witnessed the rebirth of her pre-disorder personality. It is time to feel proud that you have supported your child through this very critical time, with all its difficulties. Along with your relief at your child's health there may be a worry about stability in the future – and, more immediately, how to resume a more normal approach to eating, where your child will assume more control over the amount of food she eats.

Some children may start to falter as they approach their ideal body weight, especially if the weight has been restored quickly. They can seem less eager to eat as fear of going over an "ideal" body weight starts to worry them. If weight is being restored quickly, many parents have felt that slowing down as their child approaches normal weight is a good idea, since this is a very scary time for their children.

Remember to focus on your child achieving a healthy weight, which will mean a weight in her ideal weight range. This range is in fact pretty broad – and not the narrow "one ideal number per height" previously used by insurance companies. A healthy weight will also mean the resumption of menstruation, which will happen only when your daughter is at the right weight for her. This may in fact be a little on the low or high end of the healthy weight range, depending on what is right for her body.

This is the stage at which you will need to start helping your child regain confidence in her body's ability to choose the appropriate types and amounts of food necessary for normal growth and development. You will need to be a kind of safety net in this process. You will know best when your child is ready to be unsupervised in this. As you continue in therapy, this is one of the issues that will be discussed. In my experience, most parents feel that they know when their child is ready to take on more control over self-feeding. As tired as you may feel at this point, it is important not to rush this stage. Handing back control slowly is what seems to work best.

Most children need to relearn normal eating and hunger/fullness cues. Under your supervision, and with frequent weighing, they can slowly start to experiment with this. They will eventually get it right. Slowly allowing your child to experiment with her own hunger/fullness cues while ensuring that weight is being maintained can reassure your child that she can eat enough without eating too much. To help in this important step, I have included in this chapter an approach to eating called "intuitive eating." This information is based on the books "Intuitive Eating" by Tribole and Resch, and "The Rules of 'Normal' Eating" by Karen Koenig.

Intuitive Eating

This section defines normal or intuitive eating. As you read, you will understand normal or intuitive eating as a set of rules that uses physiology to guide when and how much to eat. It does not engage the intellect or emotion in eating decisions.

So what is normal eating? It is the ability to eat what you really want and get enough of it to feel physiologically satisfied. Sounds simple, doesn't it? It is actually how small children usually operate. They don't feel bad if they eat six cookies when they are warm and crumbly. To them it makes perfect sense. It also makes perfect sense to them to not finish dinner when they no longer feel hungry.

Normal eaters follow internal rules for eating intuitively, mindlessly really, using physiological cues to guide them. Of course as soon as we start to define "normal" and explore the rules that define it, we are no longer just intuitive eaters. If you can say, after some reflection on your inner thoughts about food, that you follow these physiological rules in your relationship with food, then you will not need to change anything in your family's eating style. However, if you are a chronic dieter or are constantly preoccupied and commenting on your weight and body shape, you will need to make some changes. In her book, "The Rules of 'Normal' Eating," Koenig has described normal eating in terms of four basic rules:

1) Eat when you are physically hungry (but not too hungry).

2) Stop eating when you are comfortably full.

3) Choose foods that you believe will satisfy you.

4) Eat mindfully and with enjoyment.

These rules seem simple and straightforward, but in fact they are very complex. There are many ways people can digress from using these "normal eating" rules. Dieting or not responding to the body's hunger cues is one way this system can break down. Routine eating beyond comfortable fullness can lead to a slow but steady weight gain. When the internal food control system has broken down, the food rules of normal eaters need to be relearned. To be fully recovered your child will eventually need to relearn these rules. It will be enormously beneficial to your child if, during the recovery process, your family can follow the rules of "normal" eating.

<u>Remember that in the immediate recovery period (during the weight gain phase of treatment) none of this applies to your child.</u> She will be eating beyond fullness and will feel bloated, especially in the beginning weeks of weight gain. You will not be ready to think about this until after significant weight restoration. As you gauge her readiness to assume control over her own food choices, you can start to describe hunger/fullness using the terminology described here. This way you will have a common language to describe normal eating. The following section explores each of the rules of normal eating in more detail.

1) Eat when you are physically hungry (but not too hungry).

The first step is knowing when you are truly hungry, and not confusing hunger with being tired, thirsty, or even bored. It means waiting until you feel the sensations of hunger fairly consistently before eating. If you eat before you are truly hungry, a normal-sized meal will make you feel too full. If you wait to eat until you are very, very hungry, you will have a hard time stopping when you are moderately full. You also won't make the best choices. If you start eating when you are consistently hungry but not ravenous, it is easier to choose healthy food, eat a normal-sized meal, and stop when moderately satisfied. In a nutshell, don't eat too soon or too late. Consistent hunger, thinking about food, a rumbling stomach, or an empty feeling are all signs of hunger. If you are irritable, unable to think clearly, or dizzy you have gone beyond moderate hunger.

2) Stop eating when you are comfortably full.

It is wonderful to leave the table feeling satisfied but not stuffed. Satisfied is feeling comfortably full. Stuffed is eating beyond that. Keep checking in as you are eating to make sure you are tuning in to the physical and psychological signs of fullness. The physical signs of fullness include a light pressure just below the waist, and a calm, more relaxed body. As you approach moderate fullness you may notice that the food seems less important. Conversation will become more important. You will feel relaxed with a sense of well-being. It takes time for this feeling of fullness to be completely registered in the brain, which is why it is important to eat slowly.

Evelyn Tribole and Elyse Resch have developed a scale, shown on the next page, that illustrates this concept. Further reading on this topic can be found in their book "Intuitive Eating." I highly recommend this book.

Hunger/Fullness Discovery Scale

From: INTUITIVE EATING BY Evelyn Tribole © 2003 by the author and reprinted by permission of St. Martin's Press, LLC.

Very hungry _____ Stuffed

1   2   3   4   5   6   7   8   9   10

1 Starving

2 Very hungry, unable to concentrate

3 Hungry, ready to eat

4 Beginning signs of hunger

5 Comfortable, neither hungry nor full

6 Comfortably full, satisfied

7 Very full, feel as if you have overeaten a little

8 Uncomfortably full, feel stuffed

9 Very uncomfortably full, need to loosen belt

10 Stuffed to the point of feeling sick

To start to learn this system, check in with your hunger during the day and pay attention to your fullness level as you eat. See what number you are when you start eating and how full you are at the end of a meal. Normal eaters will usually start eating at a 3 and usually end at a 6 or 7. When you wait until you are a 2 to eat, you will notice that you probably eat more and care less about what you eat.

It is important to remember that although normal eaters usually start at a 3 and end at a 6, this does not mean that it is wrong to sometimes stray from this guideline. There will always be times when a normal eater will not be able to eat when a 3, or will not stop at a 6 or 7. As long as these occasions are not frequent, this also is a part of normal eating. It is important to not try to model this as a perfect system. It is not perfect in that people will frequently go above or below the ideal. It is, however, a system that works, and it takes emotions and intellectual decision-making out of eating and puts food, hunger, and eating back in a physiologically based system, where they belong.

Continued weighing at this stage can reassure parents that their child's weight is not dropping, and at the same time reassure the child that her weight gain has slowed to a rate appropriate for normal growth and development. You and your child can decide what length of time you are comfortable with between weighings. I find that patients and parents often choose two weeks between weighings. As time goes on, and confidence builds about your child's ability to maintain weight, the need for these weighings will lessen.

When a child recovering from an eating disorder is relearning intuitive eating, she will need to first focus on her hunger levels. She will need to learn to eat at a 3. Waiting until she is a 2 can be triggering, as it will be a reminder of how she felt when she was restricting her intake. She has spent a lot of time at this level of hunger, and it is a place best avoided during recovery. Children vary in how quickly their normal hunger cueing returns. Practice, patience, and weight checks will help with this.

The last skill to be relearned is identifying an appropriate level of fullness needed to maintain weight. We hope this will just happen naturally. But if not, the amount of fullness needed for normal adolescent growth will need to be relearned. Sometimes a child will perceive her fullness as a 6, but still be losing weight. In this situation, she must learn how to be comfortable with a higher level of fullness. In other words, in order to maintain her weight she must learn to perceive what she believes to be a 7 as, in fact a 6. Yet again, practice, patience, and weight checks will support this final step of recovery.

Intuitive eating has other components besides recognizing physiological hunger and fullness. Normal eaters get a lot of pleasure from eating as a result of satisfying the physical sensations of smell and taste. Children with eating disorders rarely experience any pleasure from eating. Many people (without eating disorders) eat foods that should give pleasure with such guilt that they have minimized their experience of pleasure associated with eating. Despite eating an adequate amount of food, they may not feel fully satisfied. Rules 3 and 4 below, as described by Koenig, illustrate how to make sure that the food you eat is psychologically as well as physically satisfying.

3) Choose foods that you believe will satisfy you.

Honor your cravings. Following this rule takes the "should" and "should not" out of eating. There is no calorie counting, fat gram monitoring, etc. With this system, there is no bad food. All foods are allowed. Following this rule means eating without any guilt and really enjoying what you have decided your body wants. It means choosing your foods without worrying about what others will think of your choices. It means eating the cookie and not an apple if what you really want is a cookie. It means eating the chicken and pasta and not a salad if chicken and pasta are what you really want.

4) Eat mindfully and with enjoyment.

Really focus on tasting the food as you are eating it. Stay relaxed. Don't let habits of judging your food invade your enjoyment. I think one of the best ways to follow Rule 4 is to remember Rule 1. People enjoy food more and can stay more mindful if they eat when they are hungry but not too hungry. It is a good idea to eat slowly and take pauses. Normal dinner conversation should naturally create pauses. Check your hunger during the meal, not just when your plate is clean. If you are someone who eats to more than moderate fullness on a routine basis, put less on your plate initially. Go for seconds only if you are still hungry after you have slowly eaten what is on your plate.

Breaking down normal eating like this can be confusing. It will seem redundant to those of you who are normal eaters. Remember that showing normal eating by example is very important to the eating environment in which your child's recovery is occurring. Knowing the basic concepts of normal eating will help you coach your child back to the happy place of being an intuitive eater. Remember that normal eating is flexible and will break its own rules from time to time. The rules are used only to help people who have veered away from using intuitive eating as their internal guide to eating.

Why Balance Matters

This is a good place to talk about the concept of balanced meals. Although familiar to the point of being boring, balance in a meal is often underrated. By balanced, I mean a meal that has a source of protein, carbohydrate, fat, milk, and what I like to call complexity or fiber.

Before you skip on to the next section, let me explain why this balance is so important as you start practicing intuitive eating. Balance has always been described as nutritional balance. And it is true that our bodies need nutrients in the right balance to function optimally. This is of course very important but I know you have probably heard all of it before. A balanced meal also has an effect on satiety cues and can optimize your hunger and fullness sensitivity in the hours immediately after eating.

First your stomach stretches. A meal with complexity will help with this satiety sensation. Foods high in fiber such as whole grains, vegetables, fruit, beans, and nuts will all provide complexity. This is why it is a good idea, under normal circumstances, to have vegetables with meals since they are filling and will provide the stretch satiety feeling without a lot of calories. It is the same reason I don't recommend a lot of vegetables for children in the weight restoration phase of eating disorder recovery. They are very sensitive to this satiety feeling since their stomach is not used to being stretched – so denser foods must be eaten to provide enough calories while minimizing discomfort. Foods with complexity also help keep the digestive system functioning optimally and provide a myriad of vitamins and minerals.

Carbohydrates are another component of a balanced meal. Once they enter the small intestine, carbohydrates stimulate specialized receptors that start making food taste a little less tasty. Carbohydrates will also increase blood sugar and provide the best fuel for our brain (glucose). Foods such as bread, bagels, rice, pasta, corn, and fruit all contain carbohydrate that will quickly convert to glucose as it is digested. Carbohydrate foods are, therefore, immediately satisfying and will quickly stop the feeling of hunger.

Protein is another important component of a balanced meal. Many people, while eating enough protein for muscle maintenance can improve their hunger/fullness sensitivity by increasing their protein intake. Protein is a very important stimulant of the receptors in the small intestine which make the food we are eating a little less appealing. The enzymes that break down protein in the small intestine are also absorbed and will stimulate the brain to cause a feeling of fullness. Because protein is digested more slowly than carbohydrate it will delay the return of hunger. This is important for the whole family but especially for your child as she relearns body cues for hunger and fullness. Foods such as meat, eggs, cheese or a vegetable substitute such as beans or tofu are high in protein.

Fat is a much-maligned but important part of a balanced diet. Fat carries with it some very essential vitamins and fats which our body cannot make. It also significantly delays stomach emptying and can (if eaten with carbohydrate and protein) delay the return of hunger.

Milk is the last part of a healthy meal that I will discuss. Milk contains protein, carbohydrate and fat. In this way it is a naturally almost balanced food and makes an excellent addition to a meal already balanced as described above. Because the carbohydrate is in a different form to the carbohydrate found in bread etc. it will help with prolonging a feeling of fullness. It is also a great source of highly available calcium and vitamin D.

During this time, if it has not already happened, it is important to continue to persuade your child to eat her fear foods. When the push to gain weight is lessened and your child is relearning to honor hunger and fullness cues, you can add a fear food as part of a normal meal.

Your child will be more likely to stay at a healthy weight if all foods are included in her diet. A return to normal weight does not always mean that the eating disorder has gone. Some children can return to a healthy weight and still retain many of their disordered thoughts about foods. Remember, an essential part of recovery is your child's willingness or your ability to persuade them to eat these fear foods. Put in the context of a usually healthy diet and using hunger/fullness as a guide, your child will be fully recovered when all foods are neutral foods and no foods are forbidden or avoided.

Supplements

When a normal weight has been restored, it is important to make sure that any effects of the eating disorder are minimized. In this regard, I usually recommend a multivitamin supplement and a calcium supplement. The multivitamin will add Vitamin D to the diet at a level that will maximize calcium deposition in the bones. Supplements designed for women usually have higher amounts of Vitamin D and calcium than regular vitamins. These are a good choice. A calcium supplement (which usually contains approximately 500-600 mg calcium) will help boost calcium intake to a higher level. You should buy one that has Vitamin D along with calcium. Your child will still need to consume about three servings of milk or milk products per day, along with the supplements. Making up for lost time in bone development must be a priority because by the time a person is in their mid-twenties most bone building is over.

Once your child has reached a normal weight, is able to eat and enjoy previous fear foods and is using normal hunger and fullness to guide her eating you have achieved recovery and she now has tools for a lifelong healthy relationship with food. But for now you should continue in therapy to make sure that your child is developing along a healthy emotional path to adulthood.

In summary

Once your child is at a healthy weight and you feel she that can be trusted to not restrict, it is time to re-teach normal eating. This is done by explaining the rules of intuitive eating as a system where her body (not her intellect) tells her how much she should eat. Frequent weighings will provide feedback on how well she is doing.

Raising kids is part joy and part guerrilla warfare.

Ed Asner

RECIPES

BREAKFAST RECIPES

Hot Chocolate

1 cup half-and-half

1 packet Carnation Instant Breakfast

1 packet hot chocolate powder

Heat half-and-half in a microwave for 1 minute and 20 seconds. Mix in packets of Carnation Instant Breakfast and hot chocolate powder.

Milkshake

1 cup half-and-half

½ cup ice cream

1 packet Carnation Instant Breakfast

Put ingredients into blender and blend until smooth.

Optional additions – banana, strawberries, peanut butter

Oatmeal

½ cup quick oats

1 cup half-and-half

Combine oats, heavy cream, and milk in a microwave-safe bowl.

Microwave on high for 2 minutes.

Remove from microwave and mix well.

Pineapple Muffins

1 cup butter

1 cup brown sugar

2 eggs

1 small can crushed pineapple

1 mashed banana

1¾ cups all-purpose flour

2 teaspoons baking powder

1 teaspoon baking soda

½ teaspoon allspice

1 cup coconut

Preheat oven to 350 degrees.

Grease a 12-muffin pan.

Cream butter and brown sugar. Stir in eggs, pineapple, and mashed banana.

Mix flour, baking powder, baking soda, and allspice in bowl.

Add to butter mixture.

Add coconut and mix gently.

Put batter in muffin pan. Bake 20 minutes.

Muffins are tender so let cool in pans on wire rack before removing.

Breakfast Apple Raisin Bake

1/3 cup raisins

1½ cups all-purpose flour

½ cup ground walnuts

½ teaspoon salt

2/3 cup brown sugar

2/3 cup butter

4 McIntosh apples, peeled and sliced

2 eggs, beaten

1 cup sour cream

½ teaspoon cinnamon and ¼ teaspoon reserved

½ teaspoon nutmeg

Preheat oven to 375 degrees.

Boil raisins in water for 10 minutes.

Sift flour and salt into large bowl. Add ground walnuts. Reserve 2 tablespoons brown sugar. Set aside. Add remainder of sugar to flour mixture and mix well. Add butter and mix. Pack into 9-inch round cake pan. Arrange apple slices over mixture and sprinkle with 2 tablespoons brown sugar. Bake at 375 degrees for about 15 minutes, or until apples are soft.

While the above is baking, combine in a medium-sized bowl the eggs, sour cream, cinnamon, and nutmeg. Remove apple and crust mixture from oven and pour sour cream mixture evenly over the top. Sprinkle with a little more brown sugar and cinnamon. Return it to the oven to bake 30-40 minutes more. Serve warm or cooled.

Baked French Toast

1 baguette, about 24 inches

2 eggs

1 cup half-and-half

½ teaspoon cinnamon

½ teaspoon nutmeg

½ teaspoon vanilla

¼ teaspoon salt

Cooking spray

Cinnamon and sugar mixed

The night before, cut baguette into ¾-inch slices (28–30). Tightly pack into 9x13-inch baking dish.

In medium bowl whisk eggs until well blended. Add half-and-half, cinnamon, nutmeg, vanilla, and salt. Pour mixture evenly over bread. Turn bread over to soak overnight. Cover baking dish with plastic wrap and refrigerate overnight.

In the morning spray bottoms of two large baking sheets with cooking spay. Place cold, soaked bread slices on baking sheet, mopping up excess egg mixture. Spread slices out and ensure they are separated.

Bake in 425-degree oven (on middle rack) for 8 minutes. Spray top of bread with cooking spray. Turn slices over and bake 6–8 minutes.

Sprinkle with cinnamon and sugar mixture. Serve.

Breakfast Strata

1 pound breakfast sausage

2 cups sliced mushrooms

½ cup finely chopped onions

4 large eggs, lightly beaten

2 cups whole milk

1 large loaf of day-old Italian bread cut into 18–20 slices, buttered and crusts removed

1½ cups grated Swiss or Cheddar cheese

Brown sausage 5 minutes breaking it up with a fork as it cooks.

Add mushrooms and chopped onions and cook for 5 minutes stirring frquently. Set aside.

In a large bowl combine the eggs (lightly beaten) and the milk.

Place the bread in the bottom of the buttered 2½-quart casserole. Top with half the sausage mixture and ½ cup of the cheese.

Repeat with another layer of bread, the other half of the sausage, and another ½ cup of cheese.

Slowly pour the milk and egg mixture over the top and sprinkle with the last ½ cup of grated cheese.

Let the strata stand for at least an hour or cover and refrigerate for up to 24 hours.

Preheat oven to 350 degrees.

Set a baking sheet on the lowest rack of the oven to catch any drips and bake the strata until the top is nicely browned and bubbly, about 1 hour.

Corn Pudding

2 cups water

½ cup hominy grits

Salt to taste (optional)

1 tablespoon butter

1 17-ounce can of cream-style corn

½ cup yellow corn meal

3 eggs, lightly beaten

¼ cup half-and-half

4 ounces of Monterey Jack cheese, grated

1 4-ounce can of green chilies, drained and minced

Preheat oven to 350 degrees.

In a medium-sized saucepan, bring the water to a boil and gradually add the grits and salt, stirring them constantly. Reduce the heat, cover the pan, and simmer the grits, stirring them occasionally, for 25 minutes or until all the water has been absorbed.

Stir in the butter or margarine, cover the pan, and let the grits stand for 10 minutes.

Transfer the grits to a large bowl and stir in the cream-style corn, corn meal, beaten egg whites and whole eggs, milk, cheese, chilies, and cayenne. Transfer mixture to a greased 1½-quart casserole.

(If you want you can stop here and refrigerate the casserole, baking it 1½ hours before serving time.)

Bake for 1¼ hours or until a knife inserted into the center comes out clean. Let stand 10 minutes before serving.

Swiss Cheese and Egg Casserole

4 eggs, slightly beaten

1¼ cups half-and half

1¼ cups soft bread crumbs

4 ounces shredded Swiss cheese

¾ teaspoon salt

¼ teaspoon pepper

Paprika

Preheat oven to 350 degrees.

Mix all ingredients except paprika. Pour into greased 1-quart casserole. Sprinkle with paprika.

Breakfast Quesadillas

2 10-inch flour tortillas

2 tablespoons sour cream

1 cup shredded Jack cheese

2 tablespoons diced green chilies

Place tortilla on plate. Spread sour cream on a tortilla. Cover with cheese and chilies.

Cover with second tortilla. Microwave on high for 1 minute. Cut into sections with pizza cutter.

Homemade Granola (1)

(This high-calorie granola is a great choice for weight restoration.)

3 cups old fashioned oats

1¼ cups whole wheat flour

½ cup packed brown sugar

½ cup sliced unsalted almonds

½ cup chopped walnuts

1 cup dried mixed fruit, diced

¼ cup sunflower seeds

½ cup milk powder

½ cup canola oil

½ cup water

¼ cup honey

¾ teaspoon vanilla extract

1 teaspoon cinnamon

Preheat oven to 350 degrees.

Combine oats, flour, brown sugar, almonds, walnuts, dried fruit, and sunflower seeds in a bowl. Set aside.

Combine milk powder, canola oil, water, honey, vanilla, and cinnamon in a separate bowl.

Pour liquid ingredients over dry ingredients and mix thoroughly.

Place mixture on a 13x9-inch baking pan, sprayed with cooking spray. Bake until golden and crunchy, turning frequently, about 25 minutes. Cool completely. Granola can be stored in an airtight container for two weeks.

Homemade Granola (2)

One small container old-fashioned oatmeal (30 ounces)

2/3 cup wheat bran

2/3 cup oat bran

½ cup flax seed, ground

2/3 cup slivered almonds

½ cup sesame seeds

1/3 cup water

1/3 cup canola oil

1/3 cup brown sugar

Preheat oven to 300 degrees.

Pour container of oatmeal into a large bowl. Add wheat bran, oat bran, ground flax seed, slivered almonds, and sesame seeds.

Mix water, canola oil, and brown sugar in a small bowl. Add to oatmeal mixture and stir until well mixed. Pour into two 9x11-inch baking trays. Bake at 300 degrees for 40 minutes. Let cool. Store in airtight container.

European Meusli

One small container of old-fashioned oatmeal (30 ounces)

½ cup brown sugar

1 cup coconut

1 cup raisins

1 cup sliced almonds

1 tablespoon bran

Mix ingredients together and store in airtight container. Serve with cold milk.

Simple Sweet Scones

2½ cups flour

1 tablespoon baking powder

½ teaspoon salt

8 tablespoons cold unsalted butter

1/3 cup sugar

2/3 cup half-and-half

½ cup walnuts, chopped

Sugar and cinnamon for topping

Preheat oven to 425 degrees.

Put flour, baking powder, and salt into a large bowl. Mix well.

Add butter and cut in with a pastry blender or food processor, or rub in with your fingers, until the mixture looks like fine granules. Add sugar, toss to mix. Add chopped walnuts.

Add half-and-half and stir with a fork until dough forms. Form dough into a ball and turn smooth side up. Pat or roll into a 6-inch circle. Cut circle into 6 or 8 wedges.

Place wedges on an ungreased cookie sheet, slightly apart for crisp sides, or touching for soft sides. Sprinkle desired amount of cinnamon and sugar on each scone.

Bake at 425 degrees for 12 minutes, or until medium brown on top.

Pumpkin Muffins

1 cup sugar

½ cup canola oil

2 eggs

1 cup pumpkin (canned)

2 teaspoons cinnamon

1 teaspoon nutmeg

1 2/3 cups flour

½ teaspoon baking powder

1 teaspoon baking soda

Mix sugar, oil, eggs, pumpkin, cinnamon, and nutmeg together.

Mix flour, baking powder, and baking soda together and add to wet ingredients.

Stir until well blended, place in greased muffin tins. Bake at 350 degrees 20–25 minutes.

LUNCH RECIPES

Egg Salad

6 hard-boiled eggs, finely chopped

½ cup mayonnaise

2 tablespoons minced onion

2 tablespoons minced celery

Salt and pepper to taste

Pinch of curry powder (optional)

Mix and refrigerate until cold.

Basic Chicken or Turkey Salad

2 cups chicken or turkey, diced

1 cup celery

½ cup mayonnaise

Salt and black pepper

Combine and chill.

Curried Chicken or Turkey Salad

2 cups chicken or turkey, diced

¼ cup raisins

¼ cup chopped walnuts, toasted

½ cup mayonnaise

2 green onions, chopped

2 teaspoons curry powder

Combine chicken or turkey, raisins, walnuts, mayonnaise, green onions, and mix. Add curry powder and mix again. Chill.

Tarragon Chicken Salad

3 pounds boneless chicken, cooked and cut into bite-sized pieces

½ cup dairy sour cream

½ cup mayonnaise

2 celery stalks, sliced

½ cup walnuts

1 tablespoon crumbled, dried tarragon

Salt and pepper to taste

Whisk sour cream and mayonnaise together in a small bowl and pour over chicken.

Add celery, walnuts, tarragon, salt and pepper.

Refrigerate for at least 4 hours.

Tuna Salad

1 6-ounce can tuna

½ cup diced celery or cucumber diced, seeded, and peeled

¼ cup mayonnaise

1 tablespoon minced fresh parsley

1 teaspoon fresh lemon juice

Salt and pepper to taste

Mix and chill.

Roasted Vegetables

Cut any vegetable or mixture of vegetables into julienne strips. Good choices are bell peppers, carrots, parsnips, sweet potato, and turnip. Mix with sliced onion.

Toss with canola oil to coat.

Sprinkle with cumin and paprika (about 1 teaspoon each).

Roast for one hour in 350-degree oven.

Cannellini Bean Spread

1 16-ounce can cannellini beans, drained

2 tablespoons lemon juice

1 3-ounce package cream cheese, softened

½ teaspoon ground cumin

In blender or food processor combine drained beans with remaining ingredients. Process until blended. Refrigerate for 3 hours. Spread mixture on wrap. Add meat, cheese, and/or roasted vegetables.

See Dips and Spreads Recipes (page 102) for dip recipes that can also be used as spreads in sandwiches and wraps:

Pesto Bean Dip

Guacamole

Feta Walnut Dip

Green Chili Bean Dip

SOUPS

Packaged soups can be turned into substantial meals. You just need to add some high-calorie items such as canned beans such as kidney, lentils, chickpeas, etc. Always have some in the fridge. They last approximately 4–5 days when opened.

Have a container of brown rice precooked in the fridge. It will last approximately 5 days.

Cooked pasta will add calories to your soups.

Half an avocado, ½ cup of cooked brown rice, and fresh squeezed lemon juice goes great in black bean soup mix. Sour cream can also be mixed in and complements the taste as well as adding calories.

SNACK RECIPES

Nachos & Cheese

Spread 25 tortilla chips on a plate or pan. Sprinkle with 2 ounces of grated cheese and melt in microwave.

Serve with salsa.

Trail Mix

¾ cup cashews

1 cup walnuts

1 cup raisins

¾ cup peanuts

¾ cup shredded coconut

¾ cup chocolate chips

Mix all ingredients in large bowl. Store in airtight container.

Sue's Coconut Bars

2/3 cup unsalted butter

2 cups graham cracker crumbs

6 ounces semi-sweet chocolate chips

14 ounces sweetened condensed milk

1 cup chopped walnuts

1 cup coconut

Preheat oven to 350 degrees.

Melt butter. Place graham cracker crumbs in a bowl and add melted butter. Press into 9x9-inch baking pan and place in oven for 8 minutes.

Remove from oven. Sprinkle chocolate chips over top. Pour condensed milk over and sprinkle with a layer of nuts and a layer of coconut.

Bake 15 minutes, or until coconut is golden. When cooled, cut into bars. Refrigerate for 30 minutes.

Pumpkin Bread

2/3 cup butter

2-2/3 cup brown sugar

4 eggs

1 15-ounce can pumpkin

2/3 cup water

3-1/3 cup flour

2 teaspoons baking soda

1 teaspoon salt

½ teaspoon baking powder

1 teaspoon cinnamon

1 teaspoon ground cloves

1 teaspoon nutmeg

Preheat oven to 350 degrees.

Grease two 9x5-inch loaf pans. Cream together butter and sugar. Add eggs, pumpkin, and water.

Add flour, baking soda, salt, baking powder, cinnamon, cloves, and nutmeg. Mix well.

Pour into loaf pans. Bake 65–75 minutes. Makes 2 loaves.

Nutty Chocolate Granola Bars

3 cups rolled oats

1 cup chopped almonds

1 cup raisins

½ cup finely chopped walnuts

1 cup chocolate chips

10 ounces sweetened condensed milk

½ cup melted margarine or butter

1 egg

Pre-heat oven to 350 degrees.

Mix all ingredients in a large bowl. Press into a 9x13-inch greased pan. Bake for 30 minutes. When partly cooled, cut into 16 large bars.

Rice Cereal Granola Bars

½ cup salted dry-roasted peanuts

½ cup roasted sunflower seed kernels (or use more peanuts or other nuts)

½ cup raisins (or other dried fruit)

2 cups uncooked oatmeal, old-fashioned or quick

2 cups toasted rice cereal

½ cup peanut butter, crunchy or creamy

½ cup packed brown sugar

½ cup light corn syrup

1 teaspoon vanilla

Optional:

¼ cup toasted wheat germ

In a large bowl, mix together the peanuts, sunflower seeds, raisins, oatmeal, toasted rice cereal, and wheat germ, if desired. Set aside.

In a medium microwavable bowl, combine the peanut butter, brown sugar, and corn syrup. Microwave on high for 2 minutes.

Add vanilla and stir until blended.

Pour the peanut butter mixture over the dry ingredients and stir until coated.

Spoon mixture into a 9x13-inch pan. Press down firmly. Let stand for about an hour to harden, then cut into bars.

DIPS and SPREADS RECIPES

Use these on crackers, pita chips or bread, fruit, or vegetables.

Pesto Bean Dip

1 15½ –ounce can white beans

½ cup pesto sauce

½ cup cottage or ricotta cheese (full-fat)

Salt and pepper to taste

Canola oil

Drain the beans and mash very well (process briefly in food processor).

Mix in pesto and cottage or ricotta cheese.

Add canola oil as needed to moisten (should not be more than a couple of tablespoons)

Season with salt and pepper.

Cover well and chill.

Guacamole

2 ripe avocados

1 teaspoon lemon juice

2–3 cloves crushed garlic

½ teaspoon salt

Chili powder and black pepper to taste

2 tablespoons salsa

Mash avocados, add lemon juice, garlic, salt, chili powder, black pepper, and salsa. Mix. Serve with tortilla chips.

Feta Walnut Dip

1 cup crumbled feta cheese (drained)

2 tablespoons olive oil

½ cup half-and-half

1 cup chopped walnuts

Dash of cayenne

1 teaspoon paprika

Combine feta cheese, olive oil, half-and-half, and walnuts in blender. Blend on low, then medium speed.

Gradually, while blender runs at medium, add spices. Blend to a smooth paste. Chill.

Chile Verde Bean Dip

1 8-ounce package cream cheese

1 16-ounce can black beans, drained

1 4-ounce can chopped green chilies, drained

1 16-ounce jar picante sauce

2 cups shredded Mexican cheese blend

Preheat oven to 350 degrees.

In this order, layer cream cheese, black beans, green chilies, picante sauce, and grated cheese in a greased pie plate. Bake for 20 minutes.

Serve with tortilla chips or crackers.

Salmon Spread

1 8-ounce package cream cheese, softened

1 tablespoon fresh lemon juice

1 tablespoon finely chopped or grated onion

1 teaspoon prepared horseradish

1 teaspoon Mrs. Dash Original Brand seasoning

1 15-ounce can salmon

In a food processor beat cream cheese, lemon juice, onion, horseradish, dill, salt, pepper, and garlic powder at medium speed until well blended.

Drain and flake salmon, removing skin and bone.

Beat into cheese mixture at low speed until well blended.

DRINK RECIPES

Breakfast Shake

1 cup half-and-half

1 packet Carnation Instant Breakfast

¾ cup ice cream

Blend.

Fruit Breakfast Shake

¼ cup heavy whipping cream

½ banana

¾ cup strawberries (fresh or frozen)

½ cup lemon sherbet

1 packet Carnation Instant Breakfast (vanilla or fruit flavor)

½ cup whole milk

Combine all ingredients in a blender.

Blend until smooth.

Hot Chocolate

1 cup half-and-half

1 packet hot chocolate powder

1packet Carnation Instant Breakfast (chocolate flavor)

Heat half-and-half in microwave on high for 1 minute and 20 seconds. Add powders and mix well.

Chocolate-Peanut Butter Shake

½ cup heavy whipping cream

3 tablespoons creamy peanut butter

3 tablespoons chocolate syrup

1½ cups chocolate ice cream

Blend.

Strawberry Crush (nondairy)

2 cups frozen strawberries

½ cup crushed pineapple

½ cup water

½ medium banana

6 tablespoons sugar

¼ cup lemon juice

2 tablespoons honey

Blend.

Peaches and Cream

1 cup milk

1 cup canned peaches

1 cup vanilla ice cream

¼ teaspoon vanilla

Blend.

Old-Fashioned Milkshake

1 cup whole milk

1 cup ice cream

Blend.

Fruit Smoothie

1 cup yogurt (regular, with active bacteria)

1½ cup berries (raspberries, strawberries, blueberries, blackberries)

6 cubes of juice, frozen in ice cube tray (type of juice doesn't matter)

Blend until smooth.

Grape Slush (nondairy)

2 grape juice bars

2 tablespoons corn syrup

½ cup grape juice

Blend.

Orange Sherbet Shake (nondairy)

¾ cup orange sherbet

2 tablespoons corn syrup

½ cup orange juice

Blend.

DINNER RECIPES

Beef and Pork Recipes

Shepherd's Pie

1 pound ground beef

½ cup onion, diced

2 cloves garlic, minced

2 tablespoons flour

1 cup beef gravy

2 carrots, peeled and finely chopped

1 14½-ounce can corn

4 teaspoons Worcestershire sauce

1 teaspoon thyme

½ teaspoon marjoram

4 cups high-calorie mashed potatoes (see section on Side Dishes for recipes, page 153)

Preheat oven to 350 degrees.

Cook beef with onions and garlic over medium heat until brown in skillet. Add flour and stir for 2 minutes.

Add gravy, carrots, corn, Worcestershire, thyme, and marjoram.

Simmer for 20 minutes, stirring occasionally.

Spoon beef mixture into a small baking dish.

Spoon mashed potatoes over top of beef mixture.

Bake until heated through and golden brown, approximately 25 minutes.

Let stand for 5 minutes before serving.

Chili/Cornbread Casserole

2 tablespoons canola oil

½ cup onion, chopped

1 clove of garlic, minced

¼ teaspoon ground cumin

1 tablespoon chili powder

1 teaspoon unsweetened cocoa

¼ teaspoon ground cinnamon

1 pound ground beef

1 16-ounce can red kidney beans, drained

1 14½-ounce can diced tomatoes, drained

2 cups Cheddar cheese, shredded

Cornbread Topping

1¼ cups flour

¾ cup cornmeal

¼ cup sugar

2 teaspoons baking powder

½ teaspoon salt

1/3 cup heavy cream (or half-and-half)

1 egg

¼ cup sour cream

1 8½-ounce can creamed corn

Preheat oven to 350 degrees.

In medium skillet, sauté onion and garlic in canola oil over medium heat. Cook about 10 minutes until tender but not brown. Add cumin, chili powder, cocoa, and cinnamon.

Add ground beef and cook at medium-high heat. Cook meat until browned. Add red kidney beans and tomatoes to meat mixture and remove from heat.

Spoon beef mixture into a greased 2-quart casserole dish. Spread shredded Cheddar cheese on top of meat.

In a separate bowl, mix flour, cornmeal, sugar, baking powder, and salt. Add cream, egg, sour cream, and creamed corn. Mix well. Pour cornbread batter over top of meat and cheese. Spread batter evenly.

Bake for 40 minutes or until top of cornbread is golden brown.

Italian Burger

6 ounces ground beef

4 ounces sweet Italian sausage, casing removed

2 tablespoons onion, finely chopped

½ teaspoon Italian herb seasoning

4 1-ounce slices whole-milk mozzarella cheese

1 tablespoon olive oil

2 sourdough hamburger buns

¼ cup warm pizza sauce, store-bought or already prepared

Combine beef, Italian sausage, onion, and Italian herb seasoning in a bowl.

Form two patties about 1 inch thick. Grill.

Top each burger with 2 slices of mozzarella about 30 seconds before removing burgers from the grill.

Brush olive oil on the inside of each hamburger bun and lightly toast on grill until golden.

Put 1/8 cup of warm pizza sauce in each hamburger bun. Then place the burger in the bun.

Hamburger Stroganoff

¼ cup butter

1 pound ground beef

1 tablespoon flour

¼ cup chopped onion

½ pound fresh mushrooms, chopped

1 teaspoon salt

¼ teaspoon pepper

1 teaspoon Worcestershire sauce

1 cup sour cream

Melt butter in a large skillet and brown ground beef. Slowly mix in flour.

Add chopped onions, mushrooms, salt, pepper, and Worcestershire sauce. Cover and let simmer for about 15 minutes or until mushrooms and onions are soft. Add sour cream and mix well.

Serve over noodles.

Meat Loaf

2 pounds minced beef

1 onion, chopped

Salt and pepper

2 egg, beaten

1 cup soft bread crumbs

½ cup milk

1 teaspoon dried thyme

½ can condensed tomato soup

½ can water

Preheat oven to 350 degrees.

Mix together beef, onion, salt and pepper, egg, bread crumbs, milk and thyme. Place in loaf pan.

Pour over it ½ can tomato soup mixed with ½ can water.

Bake for 90 minutes.

Ribs in Barbecue Sauce
(slow cooker recipe)

3 pounds pork back ribs (2 racks)

3 cups barbecue sauce

Put ribs and barbecue sauce in slow cooker, cook on low 8–10 hours. Serve with rice.

Baked Beef Curry with Custard Topping

1½ pounds ground beef

1 cup soft bread crumbs

1 cup whole milk

1 egg

1 medium onion, chopped

½ cup slivered almonds

½ cup raisins

1 tablespoon lemon juice

2 teaspoons cumin powder

1½ teaspoons salt

¼ teaspoon pepper

2 eggs, beaten

1 cup whole milk

Paprika

Preheat oven to 325 degrees.

Mix beef, bread crumbs, milk, egg, onion, almonds, raisins, lemon juice, cumin powder, salt and pepper.

Spread mixture in ungreased 2-quart casserole. Cook uncovered for 45 minutes; drain excess fat.

Mix beaten eggs and 1 cup milk; pour over beef mixture. Sprinkle with paprika.

Place casserole in 13x9-inch pan. Pour very hot water (1 inch) into pan. Cook uncovered until beef is done and custard is set, about 30 minutes. Cut into wedges to serve.

Sweet and Sour Meatballs

Meatballs

2 cups breadcrumbs (5 slices bread)

1 egg

½ cup milk

1 pound ground beef

1 pound ground pork

1½ teaspoons salt

¼ teaspoon pepper

¼ teaspoon garlic salt

2 teaspoons of chopped fresh ginger or ½ teaspoon dried ginger

4 tablespoons soy sauce

Sauce

1 7¼-ounce can tomato sauce

2/3 cup white vinegar

2/3 cup brown sugar

1 teaspoon salt

4 teaspoons soy sauce

1 14-ounce can pineapple chunks and juice

1 teaspoon salt

2 cloves garlic, chopped

1 cup water

2 carrots, peeled and chopped on the diagonal

1 green pepper, chopped

¼ cup water

4 tablespoons cornstarch

Preheat oven to 350 degrees.

Combine bread, egg, and milk in large bowl.

Add ground beef, ground pork, salt, pepper, garlic salt, ginger, and soy sauce. Mix well and shape into balls. Place on baking tray and bake for 20 minutes.

Mix tomato sauce, vinegar, brown sugar, salt, soy sauce, pineapple juice, garlic, and water in saucepan on stove. Heat to a simmer.

Add cooked meatballs, carrots, and green peppers, simmer on very low heat 20 minutes.

Mix 4 tablespoons cornstarch with ¼ cup water. Add to sauce and stir until thickened.

Norwegian Meatballs
(slow cooker recipe)

1½ pounds ground beef

½ pound ground pork

1 egg

1 cup mashed potatoes

½ cup dry bread crumbs

½ cup milk

1 teaspoon salt

¼ teaspoon ground cloves

¼ teaspoon allspice

¼ teaspoon ground ginger

¼ teaspoon black pepper

¼ teaspoon nutmeg

¼ teaspoon brown sugar

½ cup flour

1 cup beef broth

½ cup heavy cream

½ cup chopped parsley

Preheat oven to 400 degrees.

Combine all ingredients except flour, beef broth, heavy cream, and chopped parsley.

Blend well and shape into approximately 24 meatballs.

Roll lightly in flour, place on cooking sheet and bake for 20 minutes.

Place in slow cooker. Pour over beef broth. Cover and cook on low for 7–9 hours or on high for 2–3 hours.

Just before serving stir in heavy cream and sprinkle with chopped parsley.

Mexican Lasagna

1½ pounds ground beef

1 medium onion, chopped

1 packet taco seasoning

1½ cups salsa

8 10-inch tortillas, cut into strips

1½ cups sour cream

6 ounces Cheddar cheese, shredded

6 ounces Mozzarella cheese, shredded

In a large skillet, brown beef, onion, and taco seasoning. Drain.

Spread ½ cup salsa in a 13x9-inch pan Layer tortillas first, then half the meat, ¾ cup sour cream, half the cheese, and ½ cup salsa. Repeat layers.

Cover with foil and bake for 40–45 minutes.

Let stand for 10 minutes, uncovered, before serving.

Top with shredded lettuce, chopped tomatoes, and salsa.

Chicken Recipes

Mushroom Chicken

6 tablespoons canola oil

2 cloves garlic, minced

4 4-ounce chicken breasts

½ cup grated Cheddar cheese

1 cup mushrooms, sliced (4–5 ounces)

2/3 cup heavy cream

½ teaspoon dried tarragon

Preheat oven to 350 degrees.

Heat 2 tablespoons of canola oil in frying pan. Add minced garlic and cook for 2 minutes.

Add chicken breasts and cook until no longer pink in the middle, about 20 minutes.

Remove chicken breasts and place in ovenproof dish. Sprinkle with grated cheese and bake in oven for 5 minutes.

Add 4 remaining tablespoons of oil to frying pan and fry mushrooms for 10 minutes on medium-low heat.

Add cream and tarragon and simmer on low until cream thickens slightly, making sure to scrape the bottom of the pan.

Pour cream/mushroom sauce over chicken and serve.

Chicken Enchiladas

Sauce

1 14-ounce can green enchilada sauce

1 4-ounce can chopped green chilies

1 cup sour cream

1 cup grated Cheddar cheese

1 cup shredded Monterey Jack cheese

Mix all ingredients in a saucepan and cook on low heat until cheese is melted.

Filling

1 tablespoon canola oil

¼ cup chopped onion

1½ to 2 cups cooked, diced chicken

¼ cup pitted black olives, chopped

Sauté onions in canola oil. Combine with the remaining filling ingredients. Set aside.

12 flour tortillas

¼ cup shredded Monterey Jack or Cheddar cheese

Preheat oven to 350 degrees.

Coat a baking dish with cooking spray. Cover each tortilla with some sauce. Spoon in filling, roll up and place in dish.

Cover with remaining sauce and top with cheese. Bake 20 minutes.

The Best Saucy Chicken
(slow cooker recipe)

¼ cup vegetable oil

1 onion, chopped

4 cloves garlic, chopped

3 tablespoons tomato paste

2 tablespoons paprika

¾ teaspoons each salt and pepper

½ teaspoon ground ginger

1 cup coconut milk

1 cup chicken broth

3 tablespoons smooth peanut butter

8 chicken thighs

½ teaspoon hot red pepper (optional)

¼ cup chopped fresh coriander or parsley

Place all ingredients in slow cooker. Cook on medium for 6 hours.

Baked Chicken and Rice

4 cups diced cooked chicken

1½ cups cooked rice

1 14½-ounce can cream of chicken or cream of mushroom soup

1 cup mayonnaise

Salt and pepper to taste

1 cup shredded Monterey Jack cheese

Preheat oven to 350 degrees.

Mix chicken, rice, soup, mayonnaise, salt and pepper together in medium bowl. Place in a shallow baking pan. Top with shredded Monterey Jack cheese. Bake about 30 minutes.

Creamy Chicken Bake

4 boneless, skinless chicken breasts

1 egg, beaten

½ cup seasoned breadcrumbs

¼ cup canola oil

6 ounces mozzarella cheese, grated

1½ cups heavy cream

2/3 cup Parmesan cheese

1 teaspoon parsley flakes

Preheat oven to 350 degrees.

Dip chicken in egg. Then dip chicken in the seasoned breadcrumbs and coat evenly

Heat oil in a skillet over medium-high heat and brown chicken until it is no longer pink in the middle.

Place chicken in a casserole dish. Top each chicken piece with 1½ ounces mozzarella.

Mix together heavy cream, Parmesan, and parsley flakes.

Pour cream mixture over the chicken.

Bake for 25 minutes.

Coconut Curry Chicken
(slow cooker recipe)

8 chicken thighs

¾ teaspoons each salt and pepper

2 tablespoons canola oil

1 onion, chopped

2 cloves garlic, minced

1 cup chicken stock

1 14-ounce can coconut milk

2 tablespoons curry paste (or 3 teaspoons curry powder)

4 carrots, sliced

1 can chickpeas, drained and rinsed

3 teaspoons flour

¼ cup water

2 cups frozen peas

1 cup cashew nuts

¼ cup shredded coconut, toasted

Put chicken thighs, salt and pepper, canola oil, onion, garlic, chicken stock, coconut milk, curry paste, carrots, and chickpeas in slow cooker. Cook on medium for 6–8 hours.

Mix flour and water and add to slow cooker with frozen peas. Cook on high until thickened (about 15 minutes). Add cashews and coconut. Serve.

Indonesian Chicken in Peanut Sauce
(slow cooker recipe)

8 skinless chicken thighs

5 carrots, sliced

2 onions, chopped

2 cloves garlic, minced

2 cups chicken stock

¾ cup smooth peanut butter

¼ cup soy sauce

½ teaspoon ginger

¼ teaspoon hot pepper flakes

1 cup frozen peas

1 teaspoon white wine vinegar

2 green onions, sliced

½ cup chopped, unsalted peanuts

Place chicken, carrots, onions, and garlic in slow cooker.

In small bowl, whisk together chicken stock, peanut butter, soy sauce, ginger, and hot pepper flakes. Pour into slow cooker.

Cover and cook on low for 6 hours, or until vegetables are tender and juices run clear when chicken is pierced.

Add peas and vinegar. Cover and cook on low for 10 minutes. Serve garnished with green onions and peanuts.

Crunchy Almond Chicken

1 cup slivered almonds

1 clove garlic

1 thin slice ginger root

1 teaspoon salt

1 teaspoon paprika

¼ teaspoon ground cumin

¼ teaspoon pepper

3-pound broiler-fryer chicken, cut up

1/3 cup butter, melted

Preheat oven to 375 degrees.

Place almonds, garlic, and ginger root in blender container. Cover and blend until finely ground. Mix almond mixture, salt, paprika, cumin, and pepper.

Dip chicken into butter, roll in almond mixture.

Place chicken skin-side up in ungreased, 13x9-inch pan. Cook uncovered until thickest pieces are done, 55–60 minutes.

Chicken Paprika with Dumplings

2 tablespoons canola oil

3-pound broiler-fryer chicken, cut up

1 medium onion, chopped

1 clove garlic, chopped

1 tomato, chopped

½ cup water

½ teaspoon, instant chicken bouillon

2 tablespoons paprika

1 teaspoon salt

¼ teaspoon pepper

1 green pepper

1 cup sour cream

Dumplings (recipe next page)

Heat oil in 12-inch skillet until hot. Cook chicken over medium heat until brown on all sides, about 15 minutes. Remove chicken.

Cook and stir onions and garlic in oil until onions are tender. Drain fat from skillet.

Stir in tomato, water, bouillon, paprika, salt and pepper, loosening brown particles from bottom of skillet. Add chicken. Heat to boiling and reduce heat. Cover and simmer 20 minutes.

Add green pepper. Cover and cook until thickest pieces of chicken are done, 10–15 minutes.

Make dumplings (see recipe on next page).

Remove chicken to heated platter, keep warm. Skim fat from skillet.

Stir in sour cream into liquid in skillet, add dumplings. Heat just until hot. Serve chicken with dumplings and sour cream sauce.

Dumplings

8 cups water

1 teaspoon salt

3 eggs, well beaten

½ cup water

2 cups all-purpose flour

2 teaspoons salt

Heat 8 cups water and 1 teaspoon salt to boiling.

Mix eggs, ½ cup water, flour, and 2 teaspoons salt. Add to boiling, salted water.

Cook uncovered, stirring occasionally, 10 minutes. Drain.

(Dumplings are chewy, not fluffy and tender as in the American version).

Chicken and Sausage Bake

1 teaspoon oregano

1 teaspoon paprika

1 teaspoon garlic powder

1 teaspoon salt

½ teaspoon pepper

4 medium potatoes, peeled and quartered

4 tablespoons canola oil

3-pound chicken, cut up

1 pound Italian sausage

Preheat oven to 350 degrees.

Coat roasting pan or large casserole with cooking spray. Mix seasonings. Put potatoes in pan, drizzle with 2 tablespoons oil, and sprinkle with half the seasonings.

Arrange chicken and sausage on top. Pour the remaining oil over the meat and sprinkle with remaining seasoning.

Cover and bake for 1 hour. Uncover, turn meat, and bake uncovered for 30 minutes.

FISH RECIPES

Cod au Gratin

4 tablespoons butter

2 tablespoons flour

1 teaspoon salt

½ teaspoon pepper

2 cups milk

2½ cups cod, cooked and flaked

1 cup grated cheese

Preheat oven to 350 degrees.

Melt butter, then add flour, salt, and pepper to make a paste. Add milk and cook, stirring until thickened.

Grease 2-quart casserole, pour a little sauce in the bottom, and then place a layer of fish and sprinkle with cheese.

Repeat until all ingredients are used, ending with cheese. Bake until brown (about 30 minutes).

Salmon in Salsa Sauce

½ teaspoon cayenne pepper

¼ cup sugar

1 teaspoon dried cilantro

½ teaspoon dried basil

4 salmon fillets

4 tablespoons canola oil

1 cup salsa

1 cup sour cream

Preheat oven to 375 degrees.

Mix cayenne, sugar, basil, and cilantro. Toss salmon in the mixture until well coated.

Heat oil in a sauté pan and brown salmon on both sides. Remove salmon to a baking pan and cook in the oven until done (approximately 20 minutes).

Mix salsa and sour cream in small bowl. Pour over salmon.

(Note: pan will be very black after it is used to fry the fish. This will wash easily with hot water and soap. It is mostly burnt sugar.)

Spicy Shrimp with Coconut

¼ cup canola oil

1 pound cooked shrimp

½ teaspoon salt

1 4-ounce can chopped green chilies

3 cloves garlic

½ cup sliced green onions

1 red pepper, chopped

1 cup heavy cream

½ cup shredded coconut

1 tablespoon lime juice

2 teaspoons dried cilantro

In a skillet, heat 3 tablespoons oil. Add shrimp, season with salt and sauté one minute. Transfer to a bowl and keep warm.

Heat remaining oil, add green chilies, garlic, green onions, and red pepper. Cook until softened.

Add cream, shrimp, coconut, lime juice, and cilantro and simmer uncovered until the sauce is slightly thickened.

Serve with rice or noodles.

Shrimp and Scallop Casserole

12 ounces thin noodles, cooked and drained

2 pounds scallops

1 cup (2 sticks) butter, divided

1 pound shrimp

6 tablespoons flour

½ teaspoon salt

4 cups half-and-half

½ cup white wine

1 cup sour cream

8 ounces Swiss cheese, shredded

¾ pound mushrooms, sliced

Preheat oven to 350 degrees.

Sauté scallops in 4 tablespoons butter, about 3–4 minutes. Cook shrimp for 2–3 minutes in simmering salted water and peel.

Combine noodles, scallops, and shrimp in a 4-quart casserole.

In a saucepan, melt 6 tablespoons butter. Blend in flour and salt. Add half-and-half. Cook until thickened and add wine. Pour into noodle mixture.

Stir in sour cream and cheese. Sauté mushrooms in remaining butter and add to casserole. Bake for 25 minutes.

Fish Chowder

2 tablespoons butter

¾ cup thinly sliced onion

½ cup diced celery

2 cups boiling water

2 cups diced raw potatoes

½ cup sliced carrots

1 pound uncooked fish cut in bite-sized pieces

1½ teaspoons salt

1/8 teaspoon pepper

2 cups half-and-half

Melt butter in large saucepan. Add onion and celery and cook, stirring frequently, until transparent.

Add potatoes, carrots, salt, pepper, and boiling water. Bring to a boil. Cover and simmer until vegetables are tender (about 15 minutes).

Add fish, cover and simmer 10 minutes longer. Add half-and-half. Heat but do not boil.

PASTA RECIPES

Pesto

8 ounces fettuccine

¼ cup fresh basil leaves

1/3 cup walnuts or pine nuts

2 cloves garlic

1/3 tablespoon olive oil

½ cup Parmesan cheese

Cook fettuccine per packet directions. When cooked, cover to keep warm.

While pasta is cooking, finely chop basil, walnuts, and garlic in food processor.

Gradually add olive oil while machine is running and process until smooth. Mix in 1/4 cup Parmesan cheese. Toss with warm cooked pasta.

Sesame Pasta

1 pound pasta

3 cloves garlic, minced

1 tablespoon red wine vinegar

1 tablespoon brown sugar

6 tablespoons smooth peanut butter

¼ cup soy sauce

6 tablespoons sesame oil

2 teaspoons hot chili oil or ½ teaspoon ground hot chili powder

8 tablespoons sesame seeds, toasted and divided into 6 and 2 tablespoons

6 green onions chopped

Cook pasta per packet directions. When cooked, cover to keep warm.

Place garlic, vinegar, brown sugar, peanut butter, and soy sauce in a food processor. Process for 1 minute.

With the motor running, slowly add the sesame and hot chili oil (or powder) through the feed tube. Process until well blended.

Toss sauce with the pasta. Add 6 tablespoons of the sesame seeds, tossing to coat well. Sprinkle with the remaining 2 tablespoons of sesame seeds and green onions. Serve at room temperature.

Spinach Pesto

8 ounces fettuccini

1 9-ounce packet frozen chopped spinach, thawed

½ cup grated Parmesan cheese

1/3 cup fresh basil leaves

1/3 cup walnuts

2 garlic cloves

½ cup olive oil

2 tablespoons lemon juice

Cook fettuccini per packet directions. When cooked, co keep warm.

Drain thawed spinach well by pressing into a strainer u liquid is removed.

Combine spinach with cheese, basil, walnuts, and ga food processor or blender until mixed.

With machine running, gradually add olive oil, a little time, through feed tube, until a thick paste forms. Add l juice. Toss with warm cooked pasta.

Macaroni and Cheese

1 pound of macaroni

2 cups half-and-half

4 tablespoons all-purpose flour

4 tablespoons butter

½ teaspoon salt

½ teaspoon pepper

1 teaspoon dry mustard

2 cup grated Cheddar cheese

Dry bread crumbs

Preheat oven to 400 degrees.

Cook the macaroni until al dente, drain, and place in a casserole.

Melt the butter in a pan and add the flour to form a roux. Gradually add the half-and-half and stir until smooth.

Add the salt, pepper, dry mustard, and grated cheese. Mix well and heat, stirring until the cheese is melted and well blended in.

Pour over the macaroni in the casserole, sprinkle the top with dried bread crumbs, and bake for 15–20 minutes.

Noodles Alfredo

8 ounces egg noodles, cooked

6 tablespoons butter

1½ cups heavy cream

1 cup grated Parmesan cheese

Salt and pepper to taste

Nutmeg

Cook noodles in boiling water until soft. Drain.

In a small sauce pan, melt butter. Add ½ cup cream and boil rapidly until slightly thickened.

Add noodles to sauce and toss gently. Then add half the cheese and a half cup of the remaining cream.

Toss gently. Repeat with the remaining cheese and cream. Add a pinch of nutmeg.

Pasta with Broccoli

½ pound penne pasta

2 cups broccoli florets

1 tablespoon olive oil

½ pound ricotta cheese

½ pound shredded Mozzarella cheese

1 cup pitted kalamata or black olives

2 cups spaghetti sauce

Preheat oven to 375 degrees.

Cook pasta in a large pan of boiling water 8–10 minutes until al dente, adding broccoli during last 2 minutes of cooking.

Rinse, drain, and return pasta and broccoli to pan. Stir in oil, cheeses, and olives. Mix well.

Mix in spaghetti sauce and bake 15–20 minutes or until heated through.

Fettuccini with Lemon and Cream

1 8-ounce package medium-wide noodles

1 cup whipping cream

2 tablespoons chopped parsley

2 teaspoons grated lemon peel

Dash of salt

2 tablespoons butter, softened

2 tablespoons grated Parmesan cheese

Cook and drain noodles per packet directions.

While noodles are cooking, place cream in a wide frying pan over medium-high heat and cook until bubbling.

Add parsley, lemon peel, and salt and cook for 30 seconds.

Add hot noodles to cream mixture, turn heat to low, and toss gently.

Add butter and Parmesan and continue tossing until noodles are evenly coated.

Ziti with Three Cheeses

2 tablespoons butter

2 tablespoons flour

½ teaspoon salt

1/8 teaspoon pepper

2 cups whole milk or half-and-half

1 cup shredded mozzarella cheese

1 cup shredded Swiss cheese

½ cup grated Parmesan cheese

¼ teaspoon nutmeg

10 ounces uncooked ziti

Heat 2 tablespoons butter in 2-quart saucepan over low heat until melted. Blend in flour, salt, and pepper. Cook over low heat, stirring constantly, until smooth and bubbly. Remove from heat.

Gradually stir in milk. Heat to boiling, stirring constantly. Boil and stir 1 minute.

Stir in cheeses. Add nutmeg. Cover and keep warm over low heat.

Cook ziti as directed on package, drain.

Alternate layers of noodles and sauce mixture in ungreased 2-quart casserole.

Cook uncovered until bubbly, about 20 minutes.

Carbonara

¼ pound mild Italian sausage

¼ pound cooked ham, thinly sliced

2 tablespoons canola oil

8 ounces spaghetti

2 tablespoons butter

½ cup chopped parsley

3 eggs, well beaten

½ cup grated Parmesan cheese

Remove casings from sausages and crumble. Finely chop ham.

Over medium heat, heat oil in a wide frying pan. Add sausages and ham to pan and cook, stirring occasionally for about 10 minutes.

Cook spaghetti per package directions. Drain. Add spaghetti to hot meat mixture, then add butter and parsley. Mix quickly to blend.

At once, pour in the eggs and quickly lift and mix the spaghetti to coat with eggs. Sprinkle in the Parmesan and a dash of pepper and mix again.

Tortellini Spinach Pasta

2 packets frozen tortellini

1 28-ounce can diced tomatoes, drained

1 pound frozen spinach

2–3 garlic cloves, finely chopped

4 ounces feta cheese, cut into chunks

4 ounces grated Swiss cheese

2 cups sour cream

1 cup half-and-half

1 teaspoons salt

1 teaspoons black pepper

Preheat oven to 375 degrees.

Cook the tortellini in salted water for about 3–4 minutes, drain and put in a big ovenproof dish. Add the canned tomatoes.

Defrost the spinach, squeeze out most of the excess water. Add to the pasta/tomato mixture along with the garlic, salt, and pepper. Mix well.

In a bowl mix the sour cream and the half-and-half. Add the grated cheese and feta cheese. Pour over the dish, making sure to mix well.

Bake uncovered for 20–30 minutes.

Side Dish Recipes

Scalloped Potatoes

3 tablespoons butter

2 tablespoons all-purpose flour

3 cups half-and-half

1½ teaspoons salt

Shake of pepper

6 potatoes, peeled and thinly sliced

2 tablespoons finely chopped onion

Paprika

Preheat oven to 350 degrees.

Melt butter, add flour and stir. Slowly add half-and-half,stirring all the time to make a white sauce. Add salt and pepper.

Place half the potatoes in a greased casserole, Cover with half the onions and half the sauce. Repeat layers, cover and bake at 350 degrees for one hour. Sprinkle with paprika. Uncover and bake 30 minutes longer.

Easy Potatoes

2/3 cup water

2/3 cup heavy cream

¼ teaspoon salt

2 tablespoons butter

2/3 cup mashed potato flakes

Combine water, heavy cream, salt, and butter in a microwave-proof bowl.

Microwave on high setting for approximately 4 minutes. Remove from microwave. Stir in potato flakes to moisten.

Baked Potatoes with Pesto

4 large baking potatoes

2/3 cup heavy cream

1 chicken bouillon cube

1 teaspoon lemon juice

2 teaspoons garlic powder

2 tablespoons grated Parmesan cheese

3 tablespoons chopped fresh basil or 2 teaspoons dried basil

2 tablespoons pine nuts

Preheat oven to 375 degrees.

Scrub potatoes well and prick the skins with a fork. Rub a little salt into the skins and place on a cookie sheet. Cook for 1 hour or until the potatoes are cooked through and the skins are crisp.

While the potatoes are baking, mix the cream and bouillon in a pan and simmer over low heat for about 8–10 minutes, or until reduced by half. Stir in the lemon juice, garlic, Parmesan, and chopped basil.

Remove the potatoes from the oven and cut them in half lengthwise. Using a spoon, scoop the potato flesh into a mixing bowl, leaving a thin shell of potato inside the skins. Mash the potato flesh with a fork.

Stir prepared mixture into the mashed potato flesh, together with the pine nuts.

Spoon the mixture back into the potato shells. Return the potatoes to the oven for 10 minutes. Serve.

Sweet Potatoes

Sweet potato mixture

1 29-oz. large can of yams, mashed

1 egg, beaten

1/3 cup butter, melted

1/3 cup brown sugar

Topping

1/3 cup brown sugar

1/3 cup butter, melted

1 cup cornflakes, crumbled

1/2 cup shredded coconut

1/3 cup pecans, chopped

Heat oven to 350 degrees.

Mix together yams, eggs, butter, and brown sugar to make the sweet potato mixture. Bake for 15 minutes.

While the sweet potato mixture is baking, mix together the topping ingredients.

When the sweet potato mixture is finished baking, put the topping on the sweet potato mixture.

Bake for another 30 minutes.

Green Beans with Almonds

1½ pounds fresh, whole green beans, washed

Dressing

5 tablespoons lemon juice

½ cup olive oil

1 tablespoon red wine vinegar

½ teaspoon crushed tarragon

½ teaspoon salt, pepper to taste

2 large cloves crushed garlic

2 teaspoons prepared mustard

½ cup packed fresh parsley (or 2 tablespoons dried)

1/3 pound feta cheese, crumbled

½ cup chopped ripe olives

½ cup each: thinly sliced green and red peppers

½ cup toasted sliced or slivered almonds

Steam beans for about 5 minutes. Remove from heat and immediately rinse in cold water. Drain.

Combine dressing ingredients in a large bowl. Add beans to the dressing. Add feta. Toss. Cover tightly and marinate 2–3 hours, stirring after about 1 hour.

Add olives and sliced peppers.

Mix well, cover, and chill for at least 5 hours. Stir in almonds.

Green Herb Rice

2 tablespoons canola oil

2 cups basmati rice

1 15-ounce can coconut milk

½ cup chicken broth

1 teaspoon salt

1 bay leaf

1 teaspoon dried cilantro

1teaspoon dried mint

1 small can green chilies

Heat oil in pan, add rice and stir for 3 minutes. Add coconut milk, chicken broth, salt, and bay leaf. Bring to boil and cook until all the liquid is absorbed.

Reduce heat to very low, add cilantro and mint. Cover the pan tightly and cook the rice for 20 minutes. Add green chilies.

Remove the bay leaf and mix rice to spread the herbs evenly.

Quick Corn Bread

1¼ cups flour

¾ cup cornmeal

¼ cup sugar

3 teaspoons baking powder

½ teaspoon salt

1 egg

1/3 cup heavy cream (or half-and-half)

¼ cup sour cream

1 8½-ounce can creamed corn

Preheat oven to 400 degrees.

In a large bowl, stir together flour, cornmeal, sugar, baking powder, and salt.

In a small bowl, beat egg lightly. Stir in cream, sour cream, and creamed corn.

Pour egg mixture into dry ingredients and mix just until moistened.

Turn batter into a well-greased 8-inch square or round baking pan. Bake for 25–30 minutes or until a toothpick inserted in center comes out clean.

Cut into squares or wedges and serve warm.

SALAD RECIPES

Salads are a very popular side with children who have eating disorders. If you are serving a tossed salad, be sure to add avocado, olives, nuts, and seeds to boost the calories. In the weight restoration phase, only regular salad dressing should be served.

These are some suggestions for higher-calorie salads:

Pasta salad

Potato salad

Avocado salad

Olive and tomato salad

Rice salad

Bean salad

Spinach Strawberry Salad

16 ounces fresh baby spinach

¼ red onion, sliced

¼ pound crisp bacon, crumbled

4 ounces walnuts, chopped

1 pint fresh strawberries, cleaned and sliced

Dressing

½ cup olive oil

¼ cup cider vinegar

1/3 cup sugar

1 teaspoon celery salt

1 teaspoon prepared yellow mustard

¼ small red onion, finely chopped

Wash spinach and add onion, bacon, and walnuts.

Combine dressing ingredients. Toss with salad. Add strawberries and gently toss.

Spinach Salad

8 ounces fresh spinach, washed

6 ounces grated sharp Cheddar cheese

1 cup croutons

5–6 slices bacon, crumbled

Dressing

½ cup wine vinegar

2/3 cup sugar

1 tablespoon grated onion

1 teaspoon paprika

1 teaspoon salt

1 cup olive oil

Mix spinach, Cheddar, croutons, and bacon together in a large bowl.

To prepare dressing, warm the wine vinegar slightly. Add sugar and stir to dissolve. (Note: If you don't warm the vinegar, you will have trouble getting the sugar to dissolve.)

Allow to cool. Add onion, paprika, and salt.

Stir well. Add olive oil and blend.

Toss with salad in large bowl.

Tabouleh

1 cup bulgur wheat

1 cup water

1/3 cup olive oil

¼ cup lemon juice

1 teaspoon salt

1 teaspoon ground allspice

1 cup chopped green onions

¼ cup chopped fresh mint leaves

1 cup chopped fresh parsley

½ cup garbanzo beans (chickpeas), drained

2 tomatoes, finely diced

Bring bulgur and water to a boil in a covered pan. Immediately reduce heat and simmer covered for 5 minutes or until liquid is absorbed. Bulgur should still be crunchy.

Turn bulgur into a bowl and mix in oil, lemon juice, salt, and allspice. Cool.

Add onions, mint, parsley, garbanzos, and tomatoes. Mix together lightly. Cover and chill for at least 1 hour.

Black Bean, Corn, and Tomato Salad

1 15-ounce can black beans, drained

1 15-ounce can corn, drained, or use 1 cup cooked frozen corn

8 ounces cherry tomatoes, halved

Dressing

2 tablespoons red wine vinegar

1 clove garlic, minced

1/8 teaspoon salt

Ground black pepper to taste

5 tablespoons olive oil

¼ cup chopped fresh basil

Mix black beans and corn in a medium bowl.

In a small bowl whisk together red wine vinegar, garlic, salt, and pepper.

Gradually whisk in olive oil and basil.

Add dressing to bowl with black beans and corn. Toss.

Gently mix in tomatoes.

Pasta Salad

8 ounces penne pasta

5 tablespoons olive oil

3 tablespoons red wine vinegar

Salt and pepper to taste

½ cup finely diced red onion

½ cup pitted, marinated black olives, whole

¼ cup endame (optional)

¼ cup chopped fresh basil (or 1½ tablespoons dried)

¼ cup chopped fresh parsley (or 1½ tablespoons dried)

2 tablespoons chopped fresh mint (or 1 teaspoon dried)

2 ounces feta cheese

12 cherry tomatoes, halved

Cook pasta per package directions. Drain and add olive oil, wine vinegar, olives, endame, onion, and salt and pepper to taste. If you are using dried herbs add them now. Cool to room temperature.

Gently stir in tomatoes, fresh basil, parsley, mint, feta cheese, and tomatoes. Serve at room temperature.

Technicolor Bean Salad

1 15-ounce can garbanzo beans (chickpeas)

1 15-ounce can white kidney beans

1 15-ounce can red kidney beans

1 15-ounce can baby lima beans

1 15-ounce can black-eyed peas

1 pound of fresh green beans

½ cup oil and vinegar dressing (any type is fine as long as it is not creamy)

1 cup chopped green onions

Drain canned beans.

Trim and cook green beans until slightly crunchy. Rinse immediately in cold water.

Toss canned and fresh beans together in a large bowl. Pour in the dressing, add green onions, and toss again.

Refrigerate before serving.

French Potato Salad

2 pounds red potatoes

Dressing

6 tablespoons red wine vinegar

½ red onion, minced

2 tablespoons finely minced fresh parsley (or 2 teaspoons dried)

1 tablespoon whole-grain mustard

1 tablespoon fresh tarragon (or 1 teaspoon dried)

Salt and pepper to taste

1/2 cup olive oil

Bring large pot of salted water to boil. Add potatoes, reduce heat, and simmer for 20–25 minutes or until the potatoes are tender when pierced with a fork.

Whisk vinegar, red onion, parsley, mustard, tarragon, and salt and pepper together in small bowl.

Slowly whisk in olive oil.

Pour dressing over potatoes and toss gently. Serve at room temperature or warm.

SAUCE RECIPES

Salsa Sauce

½ cup salsa

½ cup sour cream

Mix in small bowl and serve cold.

Creamy Cottage Cheese Sauce

1 cup cottage cheese

¼ cup heavy cream

2 tablespoons grated Parmesan

2 teaspoons dried dill

Dash nutmeg

Black pepper to taste

Combine all ingredients in a food processor and puree them until the sauce is smooth.

Serve with grilled chicken or fish, or use as a pasta sauce.

Spicy Peanut Sauce

5 tablespoons creamy peanut butter

2 tablespoons fish sauce (or soy sauce)

2 tablespoons lime juice

¼ cup coconut milk

1 tablespoon honey

1 tablespoon minced fresh ginger root

2 medium garlic cloves, minced

1 teaspoon curry powder (optional)

Combine all ingredients in food processor until smooth.

VEGETARIAN RECIPES

Note: Vegan recipes are denoted with an *.

Sesame/Peanut Pasta*

3 cloves garlic, minced

1 tablespoon red wine vinegar

1 tablespoon brown sugar

¼ cup creamy peanut butter

¼ cup soy sauce

6 tablespoons sesame oil

¼ teaspoon cayenne pepper

1 pound linguine, cooked and drained

8 tablespoons toasted sesame seeds, divided

3 green onions, chopped

Place garlic, vinegar, brown sugar, peanut butter, and soy sauce in a food processor. Process for one minute.

Add cayenne pepper to sesame oil. With the motor running, slowly add the sesame oil through the feed tube. Process until well blended.

Toss sauce with the linguine. Add sesame seeds, tossing to coat well. Sprinkle with green onions.

Serve warm or at room temperature.

Broccoli/Cauliflower Cheese Soup

2 cups vegetable stock

2 cups potato chunks

3½ cups broccoli or cauliflower in bite-sized pieces, divided

1 cup chopped carrot

3 medium cloves garlic

½ cup chopped onion

½ teaspoon salt

1½ cups grated Cheddar cheese

1 to 2 cups half-and-half

¼ teaspoon ground cumin

¼ teaspoon dry mustard

¼ teaspoon black pepper

2 tablespoons canola oil

1 cup sour cream

Place stock, potato, 2 cups broccoli or cauliflower, carrots, garlic, onion, and salt in a large pot. Bring to a boil, cover and simmer 15 minutes. Let cool 10 minutes.

Place the entire mixture in the blender until smooth and creamy. Return to pot.

Turn heat to low and whisk in cheese, 1 cup of half-and-half, cumin, mustard, and black pepper. Continue to add half-and-half until soup is desired consistency.

Sauté in canola oil 1½ more cups broccoli or cauliflower in bite-sized pieces. Stir in sour cream.

Broccoli Mushroom Noodle Casserole

2 stalks broccoli

¾ pound fresh mushrooms, sliced

1 large onion, chopped

3 eggs

2 cups ricotta or cottage cheese (full-fat)

2 teaspoons ground cumin

1 cup sour cream

3 cups egg noodles

1 cup sharp Cheddar cheese, grated

½ cup bread crumbs

Paprika

Preheat oven to 350 degrees.

Sauté broccoli, mushrooms, and onion in oil until soft.

Beat eggs in a large bowl. Whisk in ricotta or cottage cheese and sour cream. Add cumin.

Boil egg noodles until slightly underdone.

Add sautéed vegetables to cheese mixture, add noodles, bread crumbs, and Cheddar. Spread into greased 9x13-inch baking pan. Top with more bread crumbs.

Bake covered for 30 minutes, sprinkle with paprika, and bake uncovered for another 15 minutes.

Chilean Squash

3 12-ounce packets frozen winter squash

1 cup chopped onion

2 cloves crushed garlic

1 teaspoon ground cumin

½ teaspoon ground coriander

3 tablespoons canola oil

½ teaspoon salt

2 cups corn

1 can chopped green chilies

4 beaten eggs

Dash of black pepper

½ teaspoon chili powder

1 cup grated Monterey Jack cheese

Preheat oven to 350 degrees.

Microwave squash for 5 minutes, stir, and microwave for 5 minutes more. Stir and microwave 4 more minutes.

Sauté onions, garlic, cumin, and coriander in canola oil until onions and garlic are translucent.

Add sauté to squash along with salt, corn, canned chilies, beaten eggs, pepper, chili powder, and cheese. Mix well.

Spread into a buttered 2-quart casserole.

Bake for 20 minutes covered, then 15 minutes uncovered.

Bean Cheese Casserole

This is a three-layer casserole with spicy, cheesy beans on the bottom, vegetables in the middle, and a crusty corn bread topping. (This recipe continues to the next page.)

1½ cups canned black beans

4 ounces (½ cup) cream cheese

1 cup sour cream

½ cup grated Monterey Jack cheese

1 tablespoon canola oil

1½ cups chopped onion

2–3 large cloves garlic

¾ teaspoon salt

½ teaspoon ground cumin

½ teaspoon dried basil

2 cups mixed vegetables cut into bite-sized chunks

2 medium-sized tomatoes, chopped

¼ teaspoon salt

¼ teaspoon pepper

¼ teaspoon oregano

¼ teaspoon basil

Preheat oven to 350 degrees.

Heat the beans to boiling, drain, and immediately cut in the cream cheese so it will melt nicely into the still hot beans. Mix in the sour cream and grated cheese, set aside.

Sauté the onions and garlic in oil for 5–8 minutes. Add this sauté to the bean/cheese mixture. Add salt, basil, and ground cumin. Mix well and transfer to a buttered 2-quart deep casserole.

In the same skillet you used to sauté the onions, pan-fry the vegetable chunks, add more oil if necessary, with salt, pepper, basil, and oregano. Cook for about 3 minutes, then add chopped tomato and stir for another 5 minutes. Spread this mixture on top of the beans.

Corn Bread Topping

1¼ cups flour

¾ cup cornmeal

¼ cup sugar

2 teaspoons baking
   powder

½ teaspoon salt

1/3 cup heavy cream

1 egg

¼ cup sour cream

1 8½-ounce can creamed
   corn

In a separate bowl, mix flour, cornmeal, sugar, baking powder, and salt.

Add cream, egg, sour cream, and creamed corn. Mix well.

Pour corn bread batter over top of meat and cheese. Spread batter evenly.

Bake for 40 minutes or until top of corn bread is golden brown.

Pesto Polenta Spoon Bread

1½ cups yellow corn meal

2 cups water

¼ teaspoon salt

5 large eggs, separated and at room temperature

¼ cup freshly grated Parmesan cheese

2/3 cup pesto sauce

1 cup cream

Preheat oven to 400 degrees.

Place cornmeal and water together in a saucepan. Mix until well blended, using a wooden spoon. Add salt. Heat this mixture until it comes to a boil. Lower heat.

Cook over low heat for 5–8 minutes, stirring frequently to prevent lumps. It will be very thick.

Remove from heat and vigorously beat in the egg yolks. Stir in the Parmesan, pesto, and cream. Transfer to a large bowl and set aside to come to room temperature. Add the cream.

Beat the egg whites until stiff but not dry. Fold them quickly but carefully into the mixture and transfer to well-buttered soufflé dish. Place in oven and cook 35–40 minutes.

Spinach Pie

1 pound frozen spinach, thawed and drained

2 tablespoons canola oil

1 large onion, chopped

2 crushed garlic cloves

2 eggs, lightly beaten

8 ounces ricotta cheese

½ cup freshly grated Parmesan cheese

Salt and pepper to taste

Pinch of grated nutmeg

Short crust pastry (enough for one pie)

1 egg, lightly beaten (for pastry glaze)

Preheat oven to 375 degrees.

Heat oil in a large heavy skillet and sauté spinach, onion, and garlic.

Remove from heat and let mixture cool slightly. Transfer to a bowl, then beat in the eggs and cheeses. Season to taste with salt and pepper. Add nutmeg.

Roll out half the dough and use to line a pie pan. Spoon in the spinach mixture, spreading evenly over the base.

Roll out the remaining dough on a lightly floured surface. Seal and trim pie. Brush with egg glaze and bake for 5 minutes.

DESSERT RECIPES

Puddings

A pudding made with an instant powder and half-and-half or light cream will make a dessert high in calories. Light cream will make the pudding thicker (and more calorie rich). In my opinion heavy cream is too thick to use when making an instant pudding.

Bread Pudding

4 eggs

¾ cup white sugar

4 cups half-and-half

1 cup heavy cream

¼ teaspoon nutmeg

1 tablespoon vanilla extract

12 ounces (about half a loaf) white bread cut into 1½-inch square pieces, with crusts removed (about 8 cups)

1 cup raisins

Cinnamon and sugar mixed.

Grease 13x9-inch baking dish.

Whisk eggs and sugar in large bowl to blend well. Whisk in

half-and-half, cream, nutmeg, and vanilla

Stir in bread and raisins and refrigerate for 30 minutes.

Preheat oven to 325 degrees.

After 30 minutes in refrigerator, place in baking dish.

Sprinkle top with cinnamon and sugar mixture. Bake for 45–50 minutes until center is almost firm. Cool for 45 minutes and serve.

Quick Crème Brule

1 tablespoon unsalted butter, softened

6 large egg yolks

6 tablespoons white sugar

1½ cups heavy cream, chilled

4 tablespoons dark brown sugar

Preheat oven to 275 degrees.

Grease six custard cups with butter and set them in a glass baking pan.

Whisk yolks until slightly thickened. Add white sugar and whisk until dissolved. Add cream and whisk.

Pour mixture into custard cups.

Set baking pan in oven and pour warm water into pan until halfway up custard cups.

Bake uncovered for 45 minutes.

Classic Crème Brule

2 cups heavy cream or half-and-half

½ cup pure maple syrup

6 egg yolks

Preheat oven to 325 degrees.

Heat cream and syrup to near boiling point.

Break yolks and stir in heatproof bowl. Slowly whisk cream/syrup into eggs.

Place ramekins in ovenproof baking dish. Pour mixture into ramekins. Pour 1 inch of water into baking pan around ramekins.

Bake until no longer jiggly (15–35 minutes depending on size of ramekins). Cool and refrigerate.

Very optional step!

Sprinkle sugar on top of each. Fire with a blow torch until melted and bubbly. Serve immediately.

Rice Pudding

4 cups cream

1 cup converted rice, rinsed and drained

½ cup granulated sugar

1 large egg

1 teaspoon vanilla

3 tablespoons raisins

½ teaspoon ground cinnamon

In a medium heavy-bottomed pot bring cream to a simmer. Add rice and sugar. Cook at a gentle boil over medium heat, stirring frequently until rice is almost cooked through but still a little chewy, about 15 minutes.

In a cup whisk egg and vanilla until smooth and pale yellow. Stir into rice mixture.

Reduce heat to medium-low. Cook a further 2 minutes, stirring constantly, until thickened. Add raisins.

Cool pudding, stirring occasionally to break up skim as it forms. Sprinkle with ground cinnamon before serving.

Crème Patisserie

2 cups milk

1-inch piece vanilla bean

5 egg yolks

¾ cup sugar

1/3 cup flour

pinch salt

Scald milk with vanilla bean and set aside.

Mix egg yolks, sugar, flour, and salt in heavy-bottomed pot.

Slowly whisk in hot milk mixture and set on medium-low heat. Whisk constantly until thick and bubbly. Do not boil.

Remove from heat, pour into ramekins for individual servings and refrigerate.

Blondies

10 tablespoons unsalted butter (at room temperature)

2 cups light brown sugar

2 eggs

2 teaspoons vanilla

2 cups flour

1 teaspoon baking powder

¾ teaspoon salt

¼ teaspoon baking soda

1¼ cups chocolate chips

Preheat oven to 350 degrees. Grease and flour a 13x9-inch pan.

Cream sugar and butter, add eggs and vanilla.

Mix flour, baking powder, salt, baking soda and add to sugar/butter mixture. Add chocolate chips.

Spread evenly and bake for 25 minutes until lightly golden. Do not overcook.

Brownies

8 squares unsweetened chocolate

1½ cups butter

6 eggs

3 cups sugar

1 tablespoon vanilla

2 cups flour

Preheat oven to 350 degrees. Grease and flour two 9-inch square pans.

Melt butter and chocolate together.

Beat eggs and add sugar gradually until thick. Stir into chocolate mixture.

Fold in flour and vanilla.

Pour into greased pans and bake for 35 minutes.

Maple Stars

1 cup unsalted butter

1 cup sugar

½ cup light brown sugar

1 egg

2 teaspoons maple extract

2¾ cups flour

2 teaspoons baking powder

¼ teaspoon salt

Preheat oven to 375 degrees.

Pulse butter, sugars, egg, and maple extract in food processor until combined.

Add flour, baking powder, and salt and pulse until combined.

Flatten into disk and refrigerate about an hour.

Roll, cut, and bake for about 12 minutes.

Cool on cookie sheets for 5 minutes before transferring to rack.

BOOKS

Eating with Your Anorexic.
Laura Collins. McGraw-Hill, 2005.

Help Your Teenager Beat an Eating Disorder.
James Lock and Daniel le Grange. Guilford Press, 2005.

Intuitive Eating, 2nd Edition.
Evelyn Tribole and Elyse Resch. St. Martin's Press, 2003.

Off the C.U.F.F
Off the C.U.F.F. (Calm, Unwavering, Firm, and Funny), from the Duke Eating Disorders Program, is a skills manual that provides the curriculum taught to parents in its group programs.

The Parent's Guide to Eating Disorders, 2nd Edition.
Marcia Herrin and Nancy Matsumoto. Gurze Books, 2007.

The Rules of "Normal" Eating.
Karen R. Koenig. Gurze Books, 2005.

Skills-based Learning for Caring for a Loved One with an Eating Disorder.
Janet Treasure, Grainne Smith, and Anna Crane. Routledge, 2007.

ONLINE RESOURCES

The Academy for Eating Disorders
www.aedweb.org
Website of national eating disorders association.

Eating Disorder Survival Guide
www.edsurvivalguide.com
Informational website on eating disorders with guidance for parents using the Maudsley Approach.

Eating Disorders Coalition
www.eatingdisorderscoalition.org
Website of national eating disorders association.

Eating with Your Anorexic
www.eatingwithyouranorexic.com
Laura Collins' (author of "Eating with Your Anorexic") website with newsletter, parent's blog, and links to eating disorder sites and resources.

F.E.A.S.T.
www.feast-ed.org
A nonprofit organization of and for parents and caregivers to help loved ones recover from eating disorders.

Gurze Books
www.gurze.net
Eating disorders resource of publications on eating disorders and body image.

Maudsley Parents Website
www.maudsley parents.org
Non-profit, parent run website for information and support.

National Association of Anorexia Nervosa and Associated Disorders
www.anad.org
Website of nonprofit eating disorders organization.

National Eating Disorders Association
www.nationaleatingdisorders.org
Website of nonprofit eating disorders association.

About the Author

Claire Norton is a registered dietitian and licensed nutritionist in Massachusetts who has spent twenty years providing care in the field of Women's and Children's nutrition. She is currently the Clinical Nutritionist at the Adolescent Health Clinic and Wesson Women's Clinic at Baystate Medical Center in Springfield, Mass. She has successfully worked with adolescents and children with eating disorders, using a family therapy approach,

CPSIA information can be obtained at www.ICGtesting.com
Printed in the USA
LVOW090014280512

283478LV00001B/102/P